The Image of Sweden in the USA

The Image of Sweden in the USA

History, events and mechanisms

Carl Marklund

Issues of Contemporary History / Samtidshistoriska frågor

Samtidshistoriska institutet
Södertörns högskola
SE-141 89 Huddinge

shi@sh.se
www.sh.se/shi

This study was commissioned by the Swedish Institutet

Originally published (in Swedish) as: *Sverigebilden i USA: Historia, händelser och mekanismer*, 2023.
Translation: Carl Marklund

Cover Image: Per Lindblom
Cover: Jonathan Robson
Graphic form: Per Lindblom & Jonathan Robson

Issues of Contemporary History /
Samtidshistoriska frågor nr 47
ISSN: 2004-8858
ISBN: 978-91-89615-47-2

Contents

Introduction....7

The Middle Way....17

Neutral or not?....23

Freedom and welfare....27

Sex, suicide and *smorgasbord*....31

The image of Sweden takes shape....35

From model country to monster country – or both?....41

Crisis and recovery – back to the future....51

Conclusion....59

References....69

Introduction

The portrayal of Sweden on the international stage has become a significant focal point in both Swedish media and public discourse. Given Sweden's status as a small, globally interconnected nation, it is unsurprising that the country places considerable importance on how it is perceived abroad. These external perceptions, whether accurate or not, can profoundly influence Sweden's diplomatic relationships, societal dynamics, and economic landscape. This emphasis is particularly relevant in today's media landscape, characterized by global interconnectedness and a growing sense of societal fragmentation, both domestically and internationally. Additionally, there has been ongoing turmoil surrounding Sweden's international image. This is evident in the surge of news coverage dedicated to this topic within Swedish media, indicating a heightened level of interest and debate, especially peaking during the so-called refugee crisis of 2015. Since then, this discourse has maintained a notably elevated level of attention compared to previous periods, persisting to the present day.[1]

The Swedish media often focuses on how the once predominantly positive perceptions of Sweden as an equitable and compassionate welfare state are now overshadowed by negative portrayals of social turmoil, organized crime, and economic disparities. These tangible societal challenges not only influence domestic discussions in Sweden but also impact how Sweden is viewed internationally. For instance, recent warnings from members of the Swedish business community highlight the interconnectedness of Sweden's internal and external images. They caution that

[1] Kungliga biblioteket, Svenska dagstidningar: https://tidningar.kb.se/?q=%22sverigebilden%22&sort=asc.

the prevalence of organized crime within Sweden, coupled with the heightened international scrutiny it attracts, poses a potential obstacle to recruiting key personnel from overseas. This underscores the intricate relationship between Sweden's domestic issues and its global reputation.[2]

Foreign perceptions of Sweden are, to some extent, influenced by domestic perspectives of Swedish society, and vice versa, although nuances may be lost in translation or overlooked due to domestic biases. For instance, Swedish concerns regarding Sweden's international image do not always align with the attention Sweden receives from foreign entities. A notable example is the discourse in the Swedish media during 2022–23 regarding how the electoral success of the Sweden Democrats and their influence on the government could potentially alter Sweden's international perception, both in terms of its society and its role as a global partner. Interestingly, while Sweden's NATO application and membership process garnered significant attention abroad, particularly among neighbouring Nordic countries, it did not generate as much debate domestically. This discrepancy highlights the disparity between how Sweden views itself on the global stage and how it is perceived by external observers.[3]

It is not unexpected that the portrayal of Sweden abroad often receives varying degrees of attention domestically. Similarly, Sweden's depiction abroad is also inconsistent. This is not a recent development. Throughout the post-war era and even earlier, Sweden has been a subject of intense international debate. Rarely is the entire spectrum of Swedish society under scrutiny. Instead, it is specific aspects or fragments of Swedish reality that intermittently capture international attention, sometimes leaving a lasting impact or broader implications over time. One such example is the discourse surrounding the "Swedish model," which

---

[2] Rågsjö-Thorell, Andreas, "Storbolagen oroliga över gängvåldets effekter på Sverigebilden: 'Svårt att locka rätt kompetens,'" *Resumé*, 2023-10-20. https://www.resume.se/alla-nyheter/morgonsvepet/storbolagen-oroliga-over-gangvaldets-effekter-pa-sverigebilden-svart-att-locka-ratt-kompetens/.

[3] Svenska Institutet, *Bilden av Sverige utomlands 2022. Årsrapport från Svenska institutet* (Stockholm: Svenska Institutet, 2023).

has seen fluctuations in prominence since the 1970s. Despite the emergence of new themes, earlier perceptions often linger, contributing additional layers to Sweden's image. This layering effect can accommodate contradictory notions, coexisting within the broader narrative. It is reasonable to assume that the focus and perspective of these depictions of Sweden are heavily influenced by the ideological and rhetorical agendas of various foreign actors who originate and propagate them. However, this straightforward premise prompts the question of whether there are overarching "mechanisms" that dictate why certain events or phenomena in Swedish society garner more attention and significance in foreign perceptions than others.[4]

This report provides an overview of Sweden's historical image spanning the past century, with a primary focus on the United States. The Swedish-American relationship has consistently held a central position in Swedish societal dynamics, encompassing diplomatic, economic, cultural, and political realms. While Germany has served as a significant trading partner throughout this period, other nations such as the UK, the Soviet Union/Russia, France, and later the EU, have also been crucial to Sweden's interests. Additionally, Sweden's deep integration within the Nordic region has led to intriguing reflections of Swedish identity within the broader Nordic consciousness, particularly at the cultural level.[5] However, despite the importance of various international relationships, the focus remains on the United States due to the enduring significance of Swedish-American relations across diverse fields over the examined period. Although there may be valid arguments for exploring perceptions of Sweden and other Nordic countries in regions such as the Global South, the decision to prioritize the study of the American image of Sweden aligns with the specific objectives of this research. The study does not aim to provide an exhaustive analysis of the entirety of

---

[4] The concept of mechanisms should be understood here metaphorically, in the sense of functions or patterns.

[5] Johansson, Martin, *De nordiska lekarna: Grannländer i pressen under olympiska vinterspel* (Huddinge: Södertörn University, 2023).

Sweden's international image, given the extensive and diverse nature of the material. Instead, the focus is on pivotal events and moments where attention towards Sweden and Swedish conditions experienced notable quantitative increases or qualitative shifts. The aim of this approach is to highlight significant turning points in Sweden's international image. Given that American public discourse often serves as a representative sample of such pivotal moments and considering the presumed importance of American perceptions for Sweden, exploring the historical image of Sweden within the United States presents itself as a logical choice. This is further justified by the resonance of American perceptions within Sweden, influencing both official representtatives and broader public debates.

However, this focus presents an intriguing methodological challenge regarding the specific determinants influencing the portrayal of Sweden, as instances of what could be termed "Sweden criticism" escalate both domestically and internationally. During periods of heightened scrutiny directed at Sweden, attention has typically centred on domestic social challenges within Sweden or Swedish stances on global matters. Consequently, perspectives critical of Sweden have been granted more prominence than during intervals when relatively favourable – or "Sweden-friendly" – views of Sweden have prevailed.[6] The period under examination saw a relatively stable and predominantly positive perception of Swedish society in the United States, serving as a backdrop against which more critical narratives have unfolded at times. Focusing on the latter runs the risk of diluting the positive overarching tone, and vice versa. The tension between these contrasting elements forms the central theme of analysis in this report: How can we decipher the interplay between a generally positive sentiment and the emergence of more negative perspectives on specific issues? What underlying mechanisms can

---

[6] Here, however, not in the sense of "Sverigevänner" ("Friends of Sweden") – members of the radical conservative milieu that self-describe themselves as "Sverigevänner" are usually highly critical of today's Sweden. Lundberg, Jonathan, *Sverigevänner: Ett reportage om det svenska nätkriget* (Stockholm: Piratförlaget, 2020).

we pinpoint as catalysts for the heightened interest in Sweden, thereby giving rise to both criticism and commendation? Furthermore, why is it that recurrent negative themes, as indicated by available surveys,[7] have not significantly altered the overall perception of Sweden in a negative direction, at least not to a considerable extent thus far?

An associated methodological challenge lies in the vastness of the American dataset, which inherently reflects the diversity of American perspectives. Against this backdrop, it is not entirely pertinent to speak of a singular "American image of Sweden." Rather, it's essential to investigate how various complementary and sometimes conflicting portrayals of Sweden have evolved in interaction with one another over time. It is worth noting in this context that the concept of a society's image is inherently diffuse and ambiguous. In discussions about Sweden's image, the term often encompasses both the media's portrayal of Sweden and the perceptions held by the public or different societal groups, alongside actual achievements in various domains. Complicating matters further is the fact that social development is largely communicated and interpreted through diverse opinions about societal progress. Images and perceptions of society become intertwined in public discourse, reflecting differing views on societal functioning, values, and beliefs. Thus, the image of Sweden is inherently political. This duality introduces ambiguity in two ways: first, in the disparity between societal perceptions and demonstrable reality, and second, in the variance between different societal perceptions. In a democratic society, the free exchange of diverse social viewpoints is fundamental. However, research indicates that globalization and digitization have contributed to increased media fragmentation and political polarization,[8] fostering cognitive dissonance, conspiracy theories, and eroding social trust. From this perspective, it is not uncommon

---

[7] Svenska Institutet, *Bilden av Sverige utomlands 2023. Årsrapport från Svenska institutet* (Stockholm: Svenska Institutet, 2024).

[8] Ryan, Alexander, *How partisan emotions and negativity shape our politics* (Sundsvall: Mid Sweden University, 2023).

for foreign images and perceptions to acquire different and potentially broader meanings than the accepted understanding that domestic debates naturally encompass diverse perceptions and opinions about the state of the nation.

The investigation is grounded in an examination of American media coverage, primarily focusing on published press articles, and the corresponding public discourse concerning Sweden and Swedish societal conditions. To contextualize the media representation of the "Sweden image," I consistently strive to correlate this reporting with actual social developments, as evidenced by well-established research findings. One rationale for selecting media sources is the assumption that they generally, albeit not always accurately, reflect both societal perceptions and achievements. The study concentrates on specific conditions and events that have influenced Sweden's image abroad during historically significant moments when attention has noticeably intensified, sparking qualified debates. In addition to press materials, the research draws upon relevant scholarly literature addressing questions and topics pertinent to Sweden's image. However, it is noteworthy that much of this literature primarily focuses on how the foreign perception of Sweden impacts the perception of the Swedish social system, rather than directly addressing the broader image of Sweden itself.[9] Moreover, there are slightly older works that, while less theoretically oriented, nevertheless offer valuable insights into the Sweden-United States relationship.[10] Some of this older literature remains relevant, particularly regarding the cultural exchanges between Sweden and the United States, in-

[9] There are a number of valuable studies, such as Svensson, Göran, "Utländska bilder av Sverige: Bespeglingar i det moderna," Ulf Himmelstrand & Göran Svensson (eds.), *Sverige - vardag och struktur: Sociologer beskriver det svenska samhället* (Stockholm: Norstedts Förlag, 1988), 139–161; Lundberg, Urban & Mattias Tydén (eds.), *Sverigebilder: Det nationellas betydelser i politik och vardag* (Stockholm: Institutet för Framtidsstudier, 2008); Werner, Jeff, *Medelvägens estetik: Sverigebilder i USA*. Vols. 1 & 2 (Hedemora: Gidlund, 2008); Andersson, Jenny & Mary Hilson, "Images of Sweden and the Nordic Countries," *Scandinavian Journal of History*, Vol. 34, No. 3 (2009), 219–228.

[10] Ohlsson, Per T., *Over there: Banden över Atlanten* (Stockholm: Timbro, 1992); Thorsell, Staffan, *Sverige i Vita huset* (Stockholm: Bonnier fakta, 2004).

cluding the reciprocal flow of popular culture through literature, music, and film. It is evident that the influence of American culture in Sweden has been asymmetrical compared to the comparatively limited impact of Swedish culture in the US. Furthermore, in addition to research exploring various forms of "Americanization" in Sweden,[11] there exists scholarship highlighting the significance of the interaction between Swedish self-perceptions and identities with foreign perceptions and identities.[12]

In recent years, there has been a burgeoning field of research focusing on nation branding and public diplomacy. This research primarily delves into the ideologies, institutions, and interests driving various states' efforts to disseminate information, cultivate positive perceptions, and mitigate negative portrayals of their respective countries on the global stage.[13] While major powers typically allocate the most resources to such endeavours, research has increasingly turned its attention to the comparatively significant efforts of smaller states in this domain. Small and peripheral states often find themselves more reliant on garnering international sympathy and understanding for their policies, as well as attracting interest and investment in their economies, compared to larger societies with more robust domestic markets, defence capabilities, and diverse linguistic and cultural land-

---

[11] O'Dell, Tom, *Culture unbound: Americanization and everyday life in Sweden* (Lund: Nordic Academic Press, 1997); Åsard, Erik (ed.), *Det blågula stjärnbaneret: USA:s närvaro och inflytande i Sverige* (Stockholm: Carlsson, 2016).

[12] On security policy, for example, see Ottosson, Sten, *Den (o)moraliska neutraliteten: Tre politikers och tre tidningars moralvärdering av svensk utrikespolitik 1945–1952* (Stockholm: Santérus, 2000); Ottosson, Sten, *Sverige mellan öst och väst: Svensk självbild under kalla kriget* (Göteborg: Statsvetenskapliga institutionen, Göteborgs univ., 2001); on cultural life, see Kylhammar, Martin, *Bland resenärer och kosmopoliter: Svensk kultur inför utlandet* (Stockholm: Carlsson, 2017).

[13] Aronczyk, Melissa, *Branding the nation: The global business of national identity* (Oxford: Oxford University Press, 2013); Pamment, James, *New public diplomacy in the 21st century: A comparative study of policy and practice* (London: Routledge, 2013).

scapes.[14] It is noteworthy that several small states, particularly in the Nordic region, consistently rank high in various surveys and indexes measuring concrete aspects of social welfare and quality of life, as well as in terms of their nation brand – that is, their international impact and positive attention in the global media. This phenomenon can, in turn, create a self-fulfilling prophecy.[15] In this report, research on Swedish nation branding and public diplomacy serves as the primary foundation for a specific type of material: official Swedish coverage of Sweden's international image. This material is particularly valuable as it effectively captures the issues deemed contentious or sensitive in terms of Sweden's international image, at least according to Swedish assessment criteria.

However, the developments within so-called successful societies are not merely newsworthy; they often garner attention because their policies across different societal domains can serve as inspiration or models for other countries to emulate. This, in turn, can elevate their international relevance – a notion that underpins research on the concept of soft power, a broad category that an increasing number of states' official representatives aim to maximize.[16] In the case of Sweden, it is evident that the idea that the country, along with other Nordic nations, has offered more or

---

[14] Clerc, Louis, Nikolas Glover & Paul Jordan (eds.), *Histories of public diplomacy and nation branding in the Nordic and Baltic countries: Representing the periphery* (Leiden: Brill, 2015).

[15] Kaneva, Nadia S., "Simulating Nations: Nation Brands and Baudrillard's Theory of Media," *European Journal of Cultural Studies*, Vol. 21, No. 5 (2018), 631–648; Viktorin, Carolin, Jessica Gienow-Hecht, Annika Estner & Marcel K. Will, *Branding in modern history* (Oxford & Berghahn Books, 2018); Gienow-Hecht, Jessica, "Nation Branding: A Useful Category for International History," *Diplomacy & Statecraft*, Vol. 30, No. 4 (2019), 755–779; Browning, Christopher, *Nation branding and international politics* (Montreal & Kingston: McGill-Queen's University Press, 2023).

[16] Influentially formulated in Nye, Jr., Joseph S., *Soft power: The means to success in world politics* (New York: Public Affairs, 2004); for an overview of its many applications and interpretations, see Marklund, Carl, "Soft Power," Audrey Kobayashi (Ed.), *International Encyclopedia of Human Geography* (Oxford: Elsevier, 2020), 291–296.

less successful solutions to various societal challenges under the umbrella concept of the "Swedish model" (or "Nordic model" and its variations) has attracted international interest and thus fostered both positive engagement and, inevitably, critical scrutiny. The Swedish model has been depicted in international social science literature as the outcome of a successful, albeit sometimes paradoxical, collaboration between the state and the market, between the public and private sectors. It is also apparent how these elements continue to complement each other within Sweden's contemporary "brand." Given that the image of Sweden can potentially stem from virtually any Swedish phenomenon, research has often focused on specific concepts deemed significant and relevant to the perception of Swedish society. Consequently, there has been a strong research emphasis on more precise concepts such as the "Nordic" and the "Swedish model," rather than broader notions like the "Nordic image" or the "Sweden image."[17]

In discussing these conditions and events, it is presumed that several factors and mechanisms played a role in influencing the image of Sweden in the United States. These contexts are thus specifically highlighted in the study. It is important to note that the depicted image does not encompass "public opinion" in its entirety but rather reflects "published opinion," as portrayed in the media, primarily in press articles. Additionally, contemporary opinion reports and surveys, some of which have been commissioned by the Ministry of Foreign Affairs over the years, contribute to this source material. This material has been generated because Swedish stakeholders recognized the necessity for it

---

[17] Much of the research that forms the basis of this report has been carried out within the framework of the project "Nordic model(s) in the global circulation of ideas, 1970–2020" led by Professor Mary Hilson at Aarhus University and funded by the Independent Research Fund Denmark under project number 8018-00023B. For preliminary research results, see Rom-Jensen, Byron Z., Andreas Mørkved Hellenes, Mary Hilson & Carl Marklund, "Modelizing the Nordics: Transdiscursive migrations of Nordic models, c. 1965–2020," *Scandinavian Journal of History*, Vol. 48, No. 2 (2023), 249–271; see also Marklund, Carl & Byron Z. Rom-Jensen, *Swedish progressivism: US debates, transatlantic circulations and Nordic models* (Abingdon, Oxon: Routledge, forthcoming).

as a foundation for informed decision-making, given the significance of foreign countries' perceptions of Sweden in shaping Sweden's international actions and strategies. For decades, international research has emphasized the importance of perceptions in international politics.[18] However, since it is evident that perceptions can be manipulated – which is precisely why they are targeted in propaganda efforts – they constitute a complex subject of research. Therefore, research tends to focus on materials that explicitly capture or convey perceptions, such as opinion polls, media reports, and parliamentary sources.

Lastly, the report delves into the influence of historical events on the present-day image of Sweden. The impact of historical narratives is examined extensively throughout the report, recognizing that images from different eras overlap and intertwine. Building on this contemporary perspective, a retrospective analysis is provided to elucidate why certain historical events are believed to have exerted a more enduring influence, shaping lasting perceptions that persist in the present-day image of Sweden.

---

[18] A classic study is Jervis, Robert, *Perception and misperception in international politics* (Princeton, N.J.: Princeton U.P., 1976).

The Middle Way: Inward and outward perspectives

A hundred years ago, as a small country in northern Europe, Sweden hardly attracted more attention in the United States than other comparable small European states. At the end of the First World War, Sweden was indeed regionally important given the new security situation in the Baltic Sea region. By Swedish standards, domestic policy in the 1920s was stormy. There was great unrest in the labour market with rapid changes of government. However, compared to the many new states that emerged in Eastern Europe after the end of the war, Sweden appeared to be a relatively calm society. Apart from media events related to anniversaries, exhibitions, state visits and notable people with ties to Sweden, Sweden and Sweden-related themes did not generate significantly more attention in the American press than could be expected, given the country's size and place in the world.[19]

But even then, the US was becoming an important stage for the global projection of Sweden. There are several explanations for this. Swedish-Americans were a large group. Like other immigrants in the multicultural United States, they were often interested in their old homeland, often critically but also nostal-

[19] Rystad, Göran, Klaus-Richard Böhme & Wilhelm M. Carlgren (eds.), *In quest of trade and security: The Baltic in power politics 1500–1990*. Vol. 2 1890–1990 (Stockholm: Probus, 1995); Biltekin, Nevra, Leos Müller & Magnus Petersson (eds.), *200 years of peace: New perspectives on modern Swedish foreign policy* (New York: Berghahn, 2022); Byrkjeflot, Haldor, Lars Mjøset, Mads Mordhorst & Klaus Petersen (eds.), *The making and circulation of Nordic models, ideals and images* (Abingdon, Oxon: Routledge, 2022); Westberg, Jacob, *Svenska säkerhetsstrategier: Från neutralitetspolitik till ansökan om Natomedlemskap* (Lund: Studentlitteratur, 2023).

gically. Although many were quickly assimilated, there was a vibrant Swedish-American culture and a continuous transatlantic exchange, with personal contacts across the ocean.[20] There was also a strong desire on the part of both Swedish and Scandinavian-American civil society to maintain contact, including through the American-Scandinavian Foundation and the National Association for the Preservation of Swedishness Abroad.[21] The United States was a rising power, an important market and an impressive as well as worrying showcase for the future and emerging modernity. It was a mental place where Swedish self-identity could be reflected and questioned.[22] After the United States sided with the Entente against the Axis powers in 1917, neutral Sweden's continued contacts with belligerent Germany received negative attention in the United States. Both the Ministry of Foreign Affairs and the American-Scandinavian Foundation suggested that a Swedish news exchange in the US should be started to counteract American scepticism towards Sweden. The American-Swedish News Exchange (ASNE) was established in New York and provided information about Sweden to the American press and vice versa. Over time, it specialized in providing easy-to-read material to a vast number of rural American newspapers interested in content that they did not have to spend a lot of resources on editing or commenting on, and that could be about design, culture and art.[23]

---

[20] Pehrson, Lennart, *The New World*. Vols. 1–3 (Stockholm: Bonnier, 2014); Hjorthén, Adam, *Border-crossing commemorations: Entangled histories of Swedish settling in America* (Stockholm: Department of History, Stockholm University, 2015); Blanck, Dag & Adam Hjorthén (eds.), *Swedish-American borderlands: New histories of transatlantic relations* (Minneapolis: University of Minnesota Press, 2021).

[21] Kummel, Bengt, *Svenskar i all världen förenen eder! Vilhelm Lundström and the allsvenska movement* (Turku: Åbo Akademi, 1994).

[22] Alm, Martin, *Americanitis: Amerika som sjukdom eller läkemedel: Svenska berättelser om USA åren 1900–1939* (Lund: Nordic Academic Press, 2002); Wallengren, Ann-Kristin, *Välkommen hem Mr. Swanson: Svenska emigranter och svenskhet på film* (Lund: Nordic Academic Press, 2013).

[23] Kastrup, Allan, *Med Sverige i Amerika: Opinioner, stämningar och upplysningsarbete: En rapport* (Malmö: Corona, 1985).

The onset of the Great Depression towards the late 1920s sparked a renewed global fascination with Sweden. As nations grappled with escalating unemployment, plummeting GDP, and soaring inflation, political radicalization became a by-product of the economic downturn. Amidst worldwide chaos, the Nordic region's stability became a captivating enigma for global social commentators, particularly in the United States. The economic crisis challenged the American ethos of capitalism, individualism, and liberalism, prompting politicians, intellectuals, and journalists to explore political alternatives. While many eyed totalitarian regimes in Italy, Nazi Germany, and the Soviet Union, their lack of democracy and opposition to business deterred most American observers. In contrast, the Nordic model, with Sweden at its helm, appeared as a potentially viable alternative, offering insights into balancing democratic values with economic stability.[24]

The Nordic countries, despite being impacted by the global depression, seemed to navigate the economic and social aftermath with less severity compared to other nations. Some attributed this resilience to the deep-rooted cultural values of the Nordic region. This notion was romanticized in the international press, where the "happy Nordic region" became a common portrayal, enhancing its positive image not just in the United States but globally. This depiction contributed to a widespread interest in the Nordic way of handling crises, drawing attention to their unique blend of social and economic policies.[25] To some, the resilience of the Nordic countries during the depression was attributed to their political landscape, marked by a strong labour movement and a

---

[24] Rodgers, Daniel T., *Atlantic crossings: Social politics in a progressive age* (Cambridge, Mass.: Belknap Press of Harvard University Press, 1998); Schivelbusch, Wolfgang, *Three new deals: Roosevelt's America, Mussolini's Italy, Hitler's Germany, and the rise of state power in the 1930's* (New York: Metropolitan Books, 2006); Patel, Kiran Klaus, *The New Deal: A global history* (Princeton: Princeton University Press, 2016).

[25] Stadius, Peter, "Happy Countries: Appraisals of Interwar Nordic Societies," Jonas Harvard & Peter Stadius (eds.), *Communicating the North: Media structures and images in the making of the Nordic region* (Farnham: Ashgate, 2013), 241–262.

tradition of brokering compromises across societal divides. This blending of modernity with tradition, and the harmonious coexistence of urban and rural life, alongside a partnership between labour and capital, garnered admiration. The American-Swedish News Exchange (ASNE), while neutral, supported this newfound positive recognition. It notably collaborated with the 1930 Stockholm Exhibition organizers, showcasing the launch of functionalism by socially conscious architects, a movement often regarded as a modern milestone in Sweden.[26] The news agency invited a group of American journalists, which resulted in hundreds of largely positive articles in the American press about Swedish "modern" architecture and design. Despite the obvious differences between the multicultural and hypermodern USA and the small state of Sweden, Sweden – or rather Swedish social planning – appeared to be an attractive alternative, not least for "progressive" Americans.[27]

American journalist Marquis W. Childs' 1936 book *Sweden: The Middle Way* played a crucial role in stabilizing the narrative of the pragmatic, modern and peaceful welfare state of Sweden.[28] For Childs, the subtitle's "middle way" simply represented the Swedish attempt to navigate between the state control of totalitarian regimes and the market fundamentalism of laissez-faire liberalism. But it was also a concept launched by Democratic President Franklin D. Roosevelt in connection with his major

---

[26] Habel, Ylva, *Modern media, modern audiences: Mass media and social engineering in the 1930s Swedish welfare state* (Stockholm: Aura, 2002); Marklund, Carl & Peter Stadius, "Acceptance and Conformity: Merging Nationalism with Modernity in the Stockholm Exhibition in 1930," *Culture Unbound. Journal of Current Cultural Research*, Vol. 2 (2010), 609–634; Tistedt, Petter, *Visioner om medborgerliga publiker: Medier och socialreformism på 1930-talet* (Höör: Brutus Östlings förlag Symposion, 2013).

[27] Östlund, David, *Det sociala kriget och kapitalets ansvar: Social ingenjörskonst mellan affärsintresse och samhällsreform i USA og Sverige 1899–1914* (Stockholm: Institutionen för litteraturvetenskap och idéhistoria, Univ, 2003).

[28] Childs, Marquis W., *Sweden: The middle way* (New Haven: Yale Univ. Press, 1936).

welfare and reform program – the New Deal.[29] It was already here that the image of Sweden – in the form of the middle way – acquired its American political charge. Childs, who had previously visited Sweden in connection with the Stockholm exhibition, emphasized that Sweden had no patent solutions to the problems of either modernity or capitalism. Instead, he pointed out how, in his opinion, the country's population and politicians expressed a pragmatic spirit of cooperation, a willingness to work together to make the best of the situation – not unlike how the concept of trust has been described in recent research as a generally important factor for positive social development.[30] This was a nod to the cultural understanding of contemporary Swedish society. But Childs also stressed the importance of the strong labour movement, the cooperative movement and, above all, social democracy. The impact of Childs' message was so great that US President Roosevelt referred to Childs' book when he sent a commission to Sweden to study the cooperative movement in the Nordic countries.[31] An international media and academic debate ensued about Sweden's political and economic system. It was not a question of for or against, but rather a nuanced discussion about what made Sweden – like the other Nordic countries – function, where concepts such as democracy, planning and pragmatic consensus dominated.[32]

The initial reception in Sweden to the West's positive feedback was mixed, with some observers initially feeling almost embarrassed. However, the perception of Sweden as a modern and

---

[29] For a discussion of Childs' book and its influence in the US, see Marklund, Carl, "Sharing values and shaping values: Sweden, 'Nordic Democracy' and the American Crisis," Jussi Kurunmäki & Johan Strang (eds.), *Rhetorics of Nordic democracy* (Helsinki: Finnish Literature Society, 2010), 114–140.

[30] Rothstein, Bo, *Grundbulten: Tillit och visionen om en liberal socialism* (Stockholm: Fri tanke, 2023).

[31] Hilson, Mary, "Consumer Co-operation and Economic Crisis: The 1936 Roosevelt Inquiry on Co-operative Enterprise and the Emergence of the Nordic 'Middle Way,'" *Contemporary European History*, Vol. 22, No. 2 (2013), 181–198.

[32] Musiał, Kazimierz, *Roots of the Scandinavian model: Images of progress in the era of modernization* (Baden-Baden: Nomos-Verl.-Ges., 2002).

secure nation soon became a key part of its national identity. This self-image, enriched by American expectations and Swedish aspirations, played a crucial role in shaping the outward-facing image of Sweden, especially as it began to embrace modern public diplomacy towards the United States. The 300th anniversary of the New Sweden colony in 1938 offered a prime opportunity to showcase both Sweden's historical roots and its contemporary industrial achievements. The Saltsjöbaden Agreement further solidified the domestic cooperation between labour and capital, a theme that was echoed in Sweden's presentation at the 1939–1940 New York World's Fair, illustrating a harmonious blend of tradition and innovation.[33]

The pavilion showcased the innovative concept of a rotating Swedish buffet, known by the exotic term *smorgasbord*. However, the portrayal of Sweden as a hypermodern society of wealth and equality starkly contrasted with the reality of poverty and inequality, especially in rural areas. This disparity was vividly captured by Ludvig "Lubbe" Nordström in his reportage book *Lort-Sverige*, published the same year as the Delaware anniversary. Consequently, opposing perceptions of Sweden, both domestically and internationally, were already evident in the 1930s, marking the initial phase of Sweden's complex image abroad.[34]

---

[33] Glover, Nikolas & Andreas Mørkved Hellenes, "A 'Swedish Offensive' at the World's Fairs: Advertising, Social Reformism and the Roots of Swedish Cultural Diplomacy, 1935–1939", *Contemporary European History*, Vol. 30, No. 2 (2021), 284–300.

[34] Nordström, Ludvig, *Lort-Sverige* (Stockholm: Kooperativa förbundets bokförlag, 1938); see also discussion in Sörlin, Sverker, *Framtidslandet: Debatten om Norrland och naturresurserna under det industriella genombrottet* (Stockholm: Carlsson, 1988); Kylhammar, Martin, *Frejdiga fremskridtsmän och visionära världsmedborgare: Epokskiftet 20-tal-30-tal genom Fem unga och Lubbe Nordström* (Stockholm: Akademeja, 1994); for a critical examination of the notion of Swedish equality, Bengtsson, Erik, *Världens jämlikaste land?* (Lund: Arkiv förlag, 2020).

Neutral or not?

Beyond their shared interest in welfare policy, Sweden and the United States found additional common ground during the early phases of World War II, with both nations initially declaring neutrality. Following Japan's attack on Pearl Harbor and America's subsequent entry into the war, there was a nuanced understanding within influential American circles regarding Sweden's stance. The American perspective on Sweden was significantly shaped by perceptions of how Swedish policies might influence the Allied war effort and the strategic positions of other Nordic countries amidst the threats from Nazi Germany and the Soviet Union. Initial efforts by Danish, Norwegian, and Finnish entities to communicate their precarious situations contributed to a broader comprehension of the vulnerabilities faced by these smaller nations, including Sweden, during the global conflict.[35]

Throughout the war, Sweden's reputation among the Allied nations suffered. Criticisms in the American press highlighted several contentious issues: the perceived inadequate treatment of German-Jewish refugees in Sweden, the notion that Sweden's admittedly sizeable support for Finland during the Winter War (1939–1940) had not been sufficient and thus inadvertently pushed Finland towards Germany, and objections to Sweden's ongoing trade with Germany, especially the export of iron ore and ball bearings, were particularly contentious points. These issues collectively contributed to a declining perception of Sweden's role during the conflict.[36] At war's end, notable Swedish business

[35] Clerc, Louis, *Cultural diplomacy in Cold War Finland: Identity, geopolitics and the welfare state* (Cham: Palgrave Macmillan, 2023).

[36] See for example Joesten, Joachim, *Stalwart Sweden* (Garden City: Doubleday, Doran and Co., Inc., 1943).

figures, like Wallenberg and Wenner-Gren, remained on the Allied blacklist for their ties to Nazi Germany. Nonetheless, there were positive moments, such as the 1943 rescue of Jewish refugees from Denmark, which earned Sweden commendation from American Jewish groups in a troubled Europe. Despite this, there was concern in Sweden over potential negative perceptions in the US affecting Sweden's post-war standing. While saving lives was the primary aim of Sweden's humanitarian efforts, there was also hope that these actions would bolster Sweden's international image.[37] Worries about Sweden's neutral stance damaging its reputation partly motivated the creation of the Swedish Institute, as historian Nikolas Glover suggests.[38]

In the post-war era, the United States emerged as a crucial platform for Sweden's efforts to showcase its cultural and intellectual contributions. Despite facing criticism during the conflict, Sweden managed to preserve a considerable amount of goodwill within American progressive communities, a legacy that dated back to the 1930s. This enduring positive perception provided a fertile ground for Sweden to reassert and expand its influence and image in the US during the rebuilding and reconciliation period following World War II.[39] From Sweden's perspective, its image abroad was deemed a valuable national asset. Upon Sweden's admission to the United Nations in November 1946, Foreign Minister Östen Undén highlighted Sweden's reputation in the US as "the country of the Middle Way" during his UN speech, praising its ability to navigate internal social challenges. Undén expressed hope that Sweden could apply this balanced approach to international matters as well, particularly significant in the

---

[37] Byström, Mikael & Pär Frohnert (eds.), *Reaching a state of hope: Refugees, immigrants and the Swedish welfare state, 1930–2000* (Lund: Nordic Academic Press, 2013); Marklund, Carl, *Neutrality and solidarity in Nordic humanitarian action* (London: Overseas Development Institute, 2016).

[38] Glover, Nikolas, *National relations: Public diplomacy, national identity and the Swedish Institute 1945–1970* (Lund: Nordic Academic Press, 2011).

[39] The Swedish social scientists and social reformers Alva and Gunnar Myrdal assumed that this would be the case in the early stages of the war. Myrdal, Alva & Gunnar Myrdal, *Kontakt med Amerika* (Stockholm: Bonnier, 1941).

nascent stages of the Cold War. He effectively connected Sweden's domestic policies of welfare and social harmony with its foreign policy of neutrality, underscoring the respectability of the former while acknowledging the complexities of the latter.[40] The notion that small and neutral nations played a unique role in the post-war global reconstruction was widely acknowledged. The nascent United Nations needed experts and staff officers who could be perceived as impartial, free from the influence of colonial powers and superpowers. Sweden, along with other small, neutral countries, was often viewed as a "champion of the global interest," a possible Swedish self-identity claimed by social scientist Gunnar Myrdal, a Swedish scholar highly active in the American academic community. This concept significantly shaped Sweden's international persona during the early Cold War period, aligning it with ideals of neutrality and impartiality in global affairs.[41]

---

[40] Andrén, Nils & Yngve Möller, *Från Undén till Palme: Svensk utrikespolitik efter andra världskriget* (Stockholm: Norstedt, 1990).

[41] For example, Gunnar Myrdal was selected by the Carnegie Corporation for a large-scale study dealing with the situation of African Americans in the United States at the time, partly on the grounds that he was Swedish and therefore assumed to have a "neutral" view of the problem. This resulting study, *An American dilemma*, has had a major impact on the civil rights movement and the fight against racism in the United States and is still today an important reference in the American debate on human rights and discrimination. There is an academic debate about the extent to which Myrdal's policy recommendations reflect Swedish social policy experience, see e.g., Jackson, Walter A., *Gunnar Myrdal and America's conscience: Social engineering and racial liberalism, 1938–1987* (Chapel Hill: University of North Carolina Press, 1990); Morey, Maribel, *White philanthropy: Carnegie Corporation's* An American dilemma *and the making of a white world order* (Chapel Hill: University of North Carolina Press, 2021).

Freedom and welfare

During the war, interest in Sweden and the Nordic region, as seen through publications and articles, experienced a decline, primarily due to the overshadowing nature of wartime events. However, the late 1940s saw a resurgence of attention towards Sweden, characterized by two dominant themes: exemplarity and peacefulness. David Hinshaw's *Sweden: Champion of Peace* (1949) emphasized Sweden's commitment to peace, while Hudson Strode, a professor from Alabama, in his work *Sweden: Model for a World* (1949), positioned Swedish society as a beacon for global emulation.[42] Naboth Hedin, the director of ASNE and a close friend of Hudson Strode, played a pivotal role in the development of Strode's book,. While ASNE did commission other works by American authors on Sweden, it faced challenges in attracting commercial American publishers, as agents reportedly believed the US book market was already "saturated" with idyllic narratives of Sweden.[43]

Despite these challenges, the New York news agency continued efforts to keep Sweden in the spotlight within American and other English-speaking media. After failed attempts to establish a Scandinavian defence union between Denmark, Norway, and Sweden in 1949, ASNE invited a group of American journalists to Sweden. Following their visit, ASNE released a detailed booklet titled "Reports on Sweden by American Newspapermen," featuring around sixty articles. These pieces highlighted Sweden's precarious geopolitical stance vis-à-vis the Soviet Union and the

---

[42] Hinshaw, David, *Sweden: Champion of peace* (New York: Putnam, 1949); Strode, Hudson, *Sweden: Model for a world* (New York: Harcourt, Brace, 1949).
[43] Kastrup, Allan, *Med Sverige i Amerika: Opinioner, stämningar och upplysningsarbete: En rapport* (Malmö: Corona, 1985).

significance of the relatively modest American Marshall Aid to Sweden. Additionally, this publicity inadvertently supported Swedish tourism, promoting exclusive travel packages like SJ's "Sunlit Nights Land Cruises" or the so-called "dollar train" to the Arctic Circle, catering to affluent American tourists.[44]

In the 1950s, Western reporting on Sweden often highlighted the strength of its armed forces, particularly the air force equipped with Swedish-manufactured fighter jets. This military capability was portrayed as evidence of Sweden's readiness to defend itself, validating the country's eligibility for American support against the Soviet Union in potential conflicts, despite its stance of neutrality.[45] While the Nordic countries adopted varied approaches to their security policies, establishing what is known as the Nordic balance, they collaborated through the creation of the Nordic Council in the early 1950s. One of the Council's inaugural endeavours was publishing *Freedom and Welfare* in 1953, targeting the burgeoning university-educated Anglo-American demographic. The publication reinforced the Nordic region as a harmonious blend of political democracy, economic liberty, societal planning, and social welfare. It argued that social welfare underpins true freedom, challenging the notion that their welfare systems were rigidly socialist. Instead, it presented a pragmatic approach to using resources for enhancing living standards and social security, reminiscent of strategies from the 1930s. This effort was partially a response to the era's McCarthyism in the United States, which vehemently opposed "socialism" amidst the Cold War's early tensions.[46]

Freedom and welfare emerged as a pivotal reference within the expanding American academic landscape. As American research institutions led in various scientific domains, they naturally

---

[44] The American-Swedish News Exchange, inc., New York, *Reports on Sweden by American Newspapermen, 1949: A Scrapbook* (New York: American-Swedish News Exchange, 1949).

[45] Silva, Charles, *Keep them strong, keep them friendly: Swedish-American relations and the Pax Americana, 1948-1952* (Stockholm: Univ., 1999).

[46] Nelson, George R. (ed.), *Freedom and welfare: Social patterns in the northern countries of Europe* (Copenhagen, 1953).

attracted Swedish scholars, fostering a vital exchange that significantly benefited bilateral knowledge transfer between Sweden and the US While the American impact on Swedish scientific activities was more pronounced, this exchange underscored the dynamic interplay of ideas and innovations between the two nations.[47] It is plausible that these Swedish outreach efforts contributed to bridging academic and public spheres in the US on the topic of Sweden. The Swedish news agency in New York capitalized on media interest and academic exchanges to release *The Making of Sweden*, a booklet that reached a broader audience than the scholarly *Freedom and Welfare*. This publication highlighted the Swedish welfare state's aim to complement, rather than suppress, the values of individualism and self-reliance, aligning with cherished American ideals. It underscored the welfare state's foundation on cross-party cooperation, labour-business collaboration, and the belief in universal basic protection as an investment in the national economy.[48]

Assessing the impact of Swedish outreach on American perceptions of Sweden is challenging. However, based on American news coverage, it appears that Swedish messages resonated positively. By the mid-1950s, previous critiques of Sweden's neutrality during World War II were overshadowed by admiration for its modern industry and comprehensive welfare system, especially as Sweden's neutrality and international contributions, notably under UN Secretary-General Dag Hammarskjöld from 1953 to 1961, gained recognition. Concurrently, a provocative

---

[47] For knowledge transfer, see Eyerman, Ron & Andrew Jamison, *On the transatlantic migration of knowledge: Aspects of intellectual exchange between the United States and Sweden, 1930–1970* (Umeå: Cerum, 1992); for academic exchange, see Åkerlund, Andreas, *Public diplomacy and academic mobility in Sweden: The Swedish Institute and scholarship programs for foreign academics, 1938–2010* (Lund: Nordic Academic Press, 2016); for policy transfer, see Rom-Jensen, Byron Z., *The Scandinavian legacy: Nordic policies as images and models in the United States*. Doctoral dissertation (Aarhus: Aarhus University, 2017).

[48] Kastrup, Allan, *The making of Sweden* (Stockholm: Swedish-American News Agency & Tiden, 1953).

narrative emerged, significantly shaping Sweden's image, especially in the US: the notion of "Swedish sin."

Sex, suicide and *smorgasbord*

This narrative, encapsulated in a 1955 *Time* magazine article titled "Sin and Sweden," sensationalized Swedish attitudes towards sex education, divorce, and abortion, framing them as moral degradation linked to welfare state expansion and social reforms. This portrayal contributed to a complex, often misunderstood international image of Sweden.[49] Brown's portrayal of Swedish society's moral landscape quickly transcended the confines of cultural conservatism, gaining traction in popular culture. This shift was significantly propelled by the films of directors like Ingmar Bergman and Federico Fellini, along with the depictions of "liberated" Swedish women by actresses Harriet Andersson and Anita Ekberg. Their work played a pivotal role in disseminating and popularizing the concept of "Swedish sin" across a global audience, embedding it into the fabric of popular cultural discourse.[50] Over time, the perception of Sweden as a place of sexual freedom became intertwined with its image as an ultra-modern, highly rational society. This blend of extreme political and sexual liberalism formed a sensational international stereotype, well-aligned with the emerging sexual revolution. It conflated Sweden's political progressivism with the comercialization of sex,

[49] Hale, Frederick, "'Time' for Sex in Sweden: Enhancing the Myth of the 'Swedish Sin' during the 1950s," *Scandinavian Studies*, Vol. 75, No. 3 (2003), 351–374.

[50] Björklund, Elisabet & Mariah Larsson (eds.), *Swedish cinema and the sexual revolution: Critical essays* (Jefferson, North Carolina: McFarland, 2016).

facilitated by Swedish laws of the era, crafting a complex and intriguing narrative that resonated globally.[51]

In the early 1960s, American fascination with Sweden soared, particularly in the lead-up to the 1960 presidential election. Reports highlighted the Democrats, under the charismatic leadership of John F. Kennedy, showing keen interest in Swedish social policies, notably the comprehensive pension reform of 1959. This reform, which suggested pension funds could underpin a more aggressive government-led investment strategy, captured the attention of a party eager for innovative approaches to social welfare.[52] The Americans were also interested in the Swedish idea of the ombudsman[53] as well as the radical Swedish legislation on gender equality.[54] Swedish public diplomacy swiftly responded to the heightened American interest. A comprehensive information campaign was launched in the US, featuring the TV series "Face of Sweden," which aired across several American networks in 1962. High-profile Swedish figures, including Prime Minister Tage Erlander and leaders from trade unions and employers' organizations, embarked on tours across the United States, advocating for the benefits of pragmatic labour-capital cooperation. However, this growing fascination with Sweden stirred apprehension among conservative and church-oriented Americans, concerned that the Democrats might adopt what was increasingly referred to as "Swedish socialism."

---

[51] Lennerhed, Lena, *Frihet att njuta: Sexualdebatten i Sverige på 1960-talet* (Stockholm: Norstedt, 1994); Arnberg, Klara, "Capital of sex: Pornography sales in Stockholm, 1965–1985," *Porn Studies*, Vol. 9, No. 1 (2021), 56–81.
[52] Rom-Jensen, Byron Z., "A Model of Social Security? The political usage of Scandinavia in Roosevelt's New Deal," *Scandinavian Journal of History*, Vol. 42, No. 4 (2017), 363–388.
[53] Rom-Jensen, Byron Z., "'A cross between Batman and a public ear:' How the United States transformed the ombudsman," Haldor Byrkjeflot, Lars Mjøset, Mads Mordhorst & Klaus Petersen (eds.), *The making and circulation of Nordic models, ideals and images* (Abingdon, Oxon: Routledge, 2022), 145–164.
[54] Rom-Jensen, Byron Z., "Enthusiastic Proselytizers: Translating the Swedish Gender Policy Model in Cold War United States," *Contemporary European History*, Vol. 31, No. 3 (2022), 401–419.

The perceived threat of Swedish socialism was taken very seriously by the Republicans. In 1960, President Dwight D. Eisenhower, addressing the nation as he prepared to leave office, referred to Sweden as "a friendly country" that had embraced socialism. He cautioned that this path led to increased alcoholism, crime, sexual immorality, and suicide, highlighting the potential dangers of adopting similar policies in the United States. This statement reflects the political climate of the time, where socialism was a contentious issue in American politics.[55] Though President Eisenhower did not explicitly name the country, both Denmark and Sweden felt implicated and strongly contested the accusations in the American media. Eventually, the stereotype of high suicide rates became predominantly associated with Sweden in American media and popular culture. Tracing the origin of this misconception is challenging, but it's evident that the empirical support was lacking. Comparative statistics available at the time indicated that Sweden's suicide rates were actually lower than those of the United States, contradicting the narrative presented by Eisenhower.[56] Despite the inaccuracy, the notion of high suicide rates dovetailed with a broader, albeit unfounded, perception of Sweden as secure yet monotonous – so monotonous, in fact, that it was humorously speculated to drive people to despair. This stereotype, while lacking in evidence, reflected the simplistic caricatures often formed about other cultures.[57]

During a private trip to Sweden in 1962, the former president expressed regret for his earlier misstatement. However, by that time, the compelling narrative of Swedes as disillusioned, suicidal,

---

[55] Hale, Frederick, "Challenging the Swedish Social Welfare State: The Case of Dwight David Eisenhower," *Swedish-American Historical Quarterly*, Vol. 54, No. 1 (2003), 55–71.

[56] Hendin, Herbert, *Suicide and Scandinavia: A psychoanalytic study of culture and character* (New York: Grune & Stratton, 1964).

[57] The notion of Swedish "boredom" was obviously a sufficiently widespread – and at least in Sweden sufficiently well known – American idea of Sweden that Gunnar Myrdal felt compelled to protest in the American press. At the same time, it could be reinterpreted in Sweden as a perfectly acceptable side effect of an otherwise safe, equal and peaceful society.

and sex-obsessed, set against a backdrop of socialism and *smorgasbords*, had already taken root in American culture. This incident illustrates how "fake news" can intertwine with existing perceptions to become deeply entrenched, acquiring a momentum and longevity that persist well beyond their original context.

The image of Sweden takes shape: Swedish model and active foreign policy

Why did a small, northern European country like Sweden captivate global interest during that period? Several factors contribute. Post-war, Sweden engaged in a strategic, long-term campaign to shape its international image, focusing especially on influencing American public opinion – a tactic leveraging the US's global dominance, the proliferation of English, and advancements in technology and communication. Although Sweden has arguably never since matched the level of positive international attention it received in the 1960s, there was a continuous effort among Swedish media and foreign service to meticulously manage and safeguard Sweden's image abroad. During the late 1950s and early 1960s, the concept of a comprehensive "Sweden image" abroad emerged in Swedish discourse as something dynamic that could be improved, endangered, or even reconstructed as necessary, reflecting the era's marketing savvy and social awareness.[58]

The escalating significance of international media and societal perceptions in determining a nation's global standing is underscored by the Swedish Ministry of Foreign Affairs' response to the diplomatic strain with the USA over the Vietnam War in the late 1960s. The press service of the Ministry initiated a systematic review of Sweden's portrayal in foreign media, particularly in

[58] Marklund, Carl & Byron Z. Rom-Jensen, *Swedish progressivism: US debates, transatlantic circulations and Nordic models* (Abingdon, Oxon: Routledge, forthcoming).

American outlets. This strategic move highlights the proactive steps taken by nations to manage and understand their international image amidst geopolitical tensions.[59] In a novel twist to public diplomacy, Swedish information campaigns abroad began to embrace, rather than refute, the notoriety of the "Swedish sin." Aligning with the 1960s' liberation movements, the sexual revolution, and gender equality campaigns, the once-controversial myth evolved into a celebrated aspect of Sweden's international and domestic identity. This approach resonated with the era's alternative youth movements, positioning the "Swedish sin" as emblematic of a progressive, liberated lifestyle, thereby integrating it into Sweden's public diplomacy narrative as a positive attribute.[60]

Sweden's emergence as a standard of comparison internationally during this period can be attributed to its exceptional performance across various sectors – economically, technically, and socially. The nation's avoidance of WWII destruction offered a comparative advantage as the global economy recovered postwar. This edge was maximized through effective collaboration between the state and market forces, evidenced by strategic labour market and industrial investment policies. Alongside the US and Switzerland, Sweden quickly rose to the top of prosperity rankings, drawing global attention. Its industry thrived internationally, and its technology was renowned for efficiency and innovation. The 1960s' growth optimism was further fuelled by Sweden's rapid modernization, welfare initiatives, and social responsibility in urban development, infrastructure, and equality reforms. Sweden also engaged in significant cooperation with the US and other Western nations across economic, technological, military, and intelligence domains. Despite the secrecy surrounding some of its achievements, Sweden competed globally in

[59] Marklund, Carl, "A Swedish *Norden* or a Nordic Sweden? Image Politics in the West during the Cold War," Jonas Harvard & Peter Stadius (eds.), *Communicating the North: Media structures and images in the making of the Nordic region* (Farnham: Ashgate, 2013), 263–287.

[60] Glover, Nikolas & Carl Marklund, "Arabian Nights in the Midnight Sun? Exploring the temporal structure of sexual geographies," *Historisk Tidskrift*, Vol. 129, No. 3 (2009), 487–510.

industrial and technological arenas, significantly enhancing its global stature.[61]

While many societies worldwide experienced expansion phases, Sweden distinguished itself through its commitment to enhanced welfare and deliberate growth strategies. This approach made Sweden's modernization efforts not just successful but exemplary, showcasing that despite its modest size, the country pursued a unique path in both domestic and international policy. This distinctiveness, recognized by a growing number of observers, positioned Sweden as fundamentally different from other Western societies. The Swedish model demonstrated, across political spectrums, that economic growth and social security could indeed coexist harmoniously.[62] Swedish social policy was seen not only as uniquely ambitious but also as exceptionally humane: Swedes were reputed to see crime, drug abuse and "anti-social" behaviour as fully understandable and manageable if only the deeper causes could be uncovered and societal stigma countered. The combination of Sweden's relative smallness and its relative success helped to elevate Sweden in the international socio-economic debate. Sweden became the archetypal welfare state, not least in American social science, and thus gained a given role as a point of comparison in research, alongside the USA, West Germany and Japan. In the increasingly intense debate on the future in the late 1960s and early 1970s, Sweden came to play the role of the prototype of modern society – a potentially

---

[61] Mörth, Ulrika & Bengt Sundelius, *Interdependence, Conflict and Security Policy: Sweden and the American Control of Technology Exports* (Stockholm: Nerenius & Santérus, 1998); Lundin, Per, Niklas Stenlås & Johan Gribbe (eds.), *Science for welfare and warfare: Technology and state initiative in cold war Sweden* (Sagamore Beach: Science History Publications, 2010); Holmström, Mikael, *Den dolda alliansen: Sveriges hemliga NATO-förbindelser* (Stockholm: Atlantis, 2011).

[62] Andersson, Jenny, *Between growth and security: Swedish social democracy from a strong society to a third way* (Manchester: Manchester university press, 2006).

universal image of the future, yet exotic and unique.[63] The Swedish welfare reforms, emphasizing gender equality, childcare, environmental concerns, and economic democracy, were viewed as bold strides towards a meticulously planned future welfare state where uncertainties are minimized. Initially, in the early 1960s, there was widespread positivity surrounding this theme. However, as more libertarian voices entered the international social discourse during the 1960s, the optimistic perspective gradually gave way to sceptical inquiries regarding the perceived uniformity of the ostensibly compassionate welfare society, sometimes depicted in certain intellectual circles as characterized by "repressive tolerance." While this notion was not exclusive to Sweden – its origins lie in American and West German social discussions – and irrespective of the accuracy of assessments concerning contemporary Sweden, the country eventually became the epitome of a welfare society. Both proponents and critics of the welfare state began making various assertions about Sweden in the global political discourse. A fundamental question arose: was this phenomenon uniquely Swedish, or could it somehow extend to other societies, either through societal evolution or deliberate adoption of Swedish policy models?

The concept of the "Swedish model" emerged as a pivotal idea in the political landscape of the Cold War era, further solidifying the somewhat paradoxical perception of Sweden as both distinct and exemplary in society.[64] The concept gained wider recognition due to its inherent ambiguity. On one hand, it denoted the collaborative approach of Swedish social partners within the Rehn-Meidner model, aimed at achieving full employment, enhanced productivity, and increased wages through a blend of active labour market policies and solidarity-based wage strategies.

---

[63] Andersson, Jenny, "Nordic Nostalgia and Nordic Light: The Swedish model as Utopia 1930–2007," *Scandinavian Journal of History*, Vol. 34, No. 3 (2009), 229–245.

[64] Mjøset, Lars, "Social science, humanities, and the 'Nordic model,'" Haldor Byrkjeflot, Lars Mjøset, Mads Mordhorst & Klaus Petersen (eds.), *The making and circulation of Nordic models, ideals and images* (Abingdon, Oxon: Routledge, 2022), 34–61.

On the other hand, the Swedish model became emblematic of Swedish society in total, often in a metaphorical sense. The book *Le défi américain* (1967) by the French journalist, politician, and social commentator Jean-Jacques Servan-Schiber played a pivotal role in popularizing this broader interpretation internationally.[65]

Servan-Schreiber portrayed the Swedish model as an alternative to American and Japanese capitalism, particularly for nations seeking an independent path amid the Cold War's influence. Historian Andreas Mørkved Hellenes notes that both Swedish diplomats and Prime Minister Olof Palme, a frequent and articulate presence on English and French-language television programs with global reach, initially viewed this interpretation of the Swedish model with scepticism.[66] Their rationale was straightforward: Swedish policymakers and representatives understood that while this conceptualization might appear positive at first, it could easily lead to inflated expectations which in their turn could result in disappointment and unwarranted criticism.[67]

---

[65] Servan-Schreiber, Jean-Jacques, *Le défi americain* (Paris: Denoël, 1967).

[66] Hellenes, Andreas Mørkved, "Tracing the Nordic Model: French Creations, Swedish Appropriations and Nordic Articulations," Haldor Byrkjeflot, Mads Mordhorst, Lars Mjøset & Klaus Pedersen (eds.), *The making and circulation of Nordic models, ideals and images* (Abingdon, Oxon: Routledge, 2022), 83–101.

[67] Marklund, Carl, "The Social Laboratory, the Middle Way, and the Swedish Model: Three Frames for the Image of Sweden," *Scandinavian Journal of History*, Vol. 34, No. 3 (2009), 264–285.

From model country to monster country – or both?

The establishment of Sweden as a harbinger of the future also prompted critical assessments of the country and its social conditions. A notable example is the publication of *The New Totalitarians* by the British-South African journalist and Stockholm correspondent, Roland Huntford, in 1971.[68] Huntford seized upon the portrayal of Sweden as an advanced welfare state that had garnered significant international attention. However, he cautioned that the outside world had overlooked the inherent undemocratic and bureaucratic tendencies within the Swedish social model. What was lauded internationally as Sweden's high standard of living and robust social security, according to Huntford, in fact served as mechanisms for extensive social control. Huntford's scathing critique of Sweden resonated widely, particularly as Sweden surpassed the USA in GDP per capita in July 1973, drawing increased scrutiny of Sweden as a potential model for other Western democracies grappling with issues such as unemployment, the energy crisis, and stagflation. This scrutiny prompted a closer examination of the true nature of Swedish society among sceptics from both the right and the left. However, alongside these factors, there were other events that brought Sweden to the forefront of the international agenda in the early 1970s, notably the Vietnam War.

---

[68] Huntford, Roland, *The new totalitarians* (London: Allen Lane, 1971); see discussion in Hale, Frederick, "Brave New World in Sweden? Roland Huntford's *The New Totalitarians*," *Scandinavian Studies*, Vol. 78, No. 2 (2006), 167–190.

In a poignant radio address in December 1972, Prime Minister Olof Palme eloquently likened the US aerial bombardments in North Vietnam to historical atrocities, invoking the names of "Guernica, Oradour, Babij Jar, Katyn, Lidice, Sharpeville, Treblinka" as points of comparison.[69] Palme's remarks displeased the Nixon administration, not least because since the late 1960s Sweden had given asylum to American deserters and draft dodgers protesting the war in Vietnam.[70] Sweden's relations with one of the world's two superpowers reached a freezing point according to diplomat Leif Leifland's assessment – a superpower on which Sweden was also heavily dependent on many levels. However, the diplomatic conflict soon subsided. But the "year of the frost" nevertheless had a lasting impact on the international image of Sweden, both in the United States and in the rest of the world: on the one hand, Sweden appeared as an advocate for the self-determination of small states and a more just world order,[71] especially in the Global South, where Palme in particular became a popular and well-known statesman.[72] Conversely, Sweden's purportedly self-assigned role of "world conscience" began to draw more critical scrutiny, even from those who fundamentally agreed with Sweden's stance. This was notably evident in the United States, where widespread disapproval of the Vietnam War

[69] The literature on Sweden's criticism of Vietnam and the American response is extensive. An overview can be found in Scott, Carl-Gustaf, *Swedish social democracy and the Vietnam War* (Stockholm: Södertörn University, 2017).

[70] Erlandsson, Johan, *Desertörerna* (Stockholm: Carlsson, 2016).

[71] Ekengren, Ann-Marie, *Olof Palme och utrikespolitiken: Europa och Tredje världen* (Umeå: Boréa, 2005); Hellenes, Andreas Mørkved & Carl Marklund, "Sweden Goes Global: Francophonie, Palme, and the North-South Dialogue during the Cold War," *Histoire@Politique. Politique, culture, société*, No. 35 (2018).

[72] Marklund, Carl, "Double Loyalties? Small-State Solidarity and the Debates on New International Economic Order in Sweden During the Long 1970s," *Scandinavian Journal of History*, Vol. 45, No. 3 (2019), 384–406.

and the Nixon administration had galvanized a significant portion of the population.[73]

In an attempt to discern the prevailing perceptions of Sweden in the United States amidst a tense period in Swedish-American relations, the Swedish authorities commissioned the market research firm Response Analysis Corporation in Princeton in the spring of 1973 to survey Americans' knowledge and attitudes toward Sweden. The findings were unexpectedly revealing: Americans, including the well-educated and influential individuals who were knowledgeable about Sweden, predominantly perceived the country as "socialist." This revelation took the Swedish clients by surprise, especially since the report did not elucidate the rationale behind such a classification – whether it stemmed from Sweden's comprehensive welfare system or a misconception equating Swedish business practices with state ownership akin to that in communist nations. Furthermore, the Americans' understanding of Sweden's neutrality was notably vague. The study also uncovered that many people's impressions of Sweden were influenced by advertising and other commercial content that exploited stereotypes around "Swedish sin," rather than a profound comprehension of the country. On a reassuring note for its Swedish clientele, Response Analysis Corporation concluded that, contrary to the apprehensions of many Swedes, particularly those with conservative views, the ideological clash between Palme and Nixon over Vietnam seemingly had no significant effect on the American perception of Sweden, as indicated by the survey results.[74]

Amidst the diplomatic strains between Sweden and the US throughout the tumultuous 1970s, it remains clear that Sweden was regarded as a part of the Western world, both domestically and internationally. By the time the survey was conducted, the

---

[73] Marklund, Carl, "From 'False' Neutrality to 'True' Socialism: Unofficial US 'Sweden-bashing' During the Later Palme Years, 1973–1986," *Journal of Transnational American Studies*, Vol. 7, No. 1 (2016), 1–18.

[74] Response Analysis Corporation, *Knowledge of and attitudes toward Sweden: Nationwide studies among the American public* (Princeton, N.J.: Response analysis corporation, 1973).

United States had already exited the Vietnam War, and a considerable number of Americans fundamentally agreed with the Swedish critique of American military actions. Apart from a temporary freeze in military cooperation, such as naval visits, and some residual uncertainty in the US regarding Sweden's foreign policy objectives, the diplomatic fallout appeared to have minimal impact on the actual exchange between the two nations. Notably, during this period, the interaction between American and Swedish research communities not only continued but also intensified, showcasing the resilience and depth of their bilateral relations.[75]

However, the study revealed that the notion of "Swedish socialism" had become deeply ingrained. This perception was soon augmented by a new, more tangible aspect in the American view of Sweden, specifically regarding its tax system and the associated bureaucratic oversight. The narrative was further fuelled by specific incidents involving individuals that captured media attention. During the spring of the 1976 election year, international media ran reports on the tax issues of two of Sweden's most celebrated cultural figures, Ingmar Bergman and Astrid Lindgren. Both leveraged their prominence to voice criticism against Sweden's marginal tax rates, their grievances gaining attention in the *New York Times* among other American publications. *Time* magazine utilized the Bergman incident as a foundation for an in-depth feature on Sweden titled "Sweden's surrealistic socialism," which also cast a spotlight on the country's bureaucratic and paternalistic tendencies.[76] Simultaneously, Sweden emerged, perhaps more distinctly than ever, as a paradigm of "democratic socialism" that was ideologically pure yet practically realized – a conspicuously defined alternative to both American capitalism and Soviet communism. The significant welfare

[75] Mays, Christin, *Have money, will travel: Scholarships and academic exchange between Sweden and the United States, 1912–1980* (Uppsala: Acta Universitatis Upsaliensis, 2022).

[76] Marklund, Carl, "Krångla lagom! Välfärdsstatskritiken och byråkratiseringsdebatten," Jenny Andersson, Nikolas Glover, Orsi Husz & David Larsson Heidenblad (eds.), *Marknadens tid: Mellan folkhemskapitalism och nyliberalism* (Lund: Nordic Academic Press, 2023), 33–53.

reforms enacted in the post-war era, along with radical concepts such as economic democracy through the so-called wage earner funds, garnered widespread attention globally, including the American left. As historian Kjell Östberg has highlighted, it prompts reflection on whether Sweden was indeed advancing towards democratic socialism during this period.[77]

The bourgeois electoral victory in 1976 was interpreted by the American press as evidence that even the Swedes had become disillusioned with "Swedish socialism." However, informed American analysts concurrently posited that the bourgeois government was likely to adhere closely to the social democratic agenda in most aspects of social policy. This perspective simultaneously underscored the intrinsic connection between modern Sweden's social framework and social democracy, while also introducing a new narrative in the discourse on Sweden – Swedish inflexibility. Where Sweden was once heralded as a beacon of innovative experimentation, American commentators – predominantly from the right and linked to the burgeoning neoliberal discourse – began to critique Sweden for its perceived stagnation and failure to enact necessary economic reforms. This critique quickly resonated within Sweden itself: during the tumultuous late 1970s, it became a common viewpoint among Swedish social commentators that the nation had diminished in international stature. This perception likely mirrored an escalating domestic apprehension regarding social progress and a national uncertainty about the sustainability of the "Swedish model" in facing heightened global competition and maintaining its ranking in terms of prosperity.[78] Marquis W. Childs returned to Sweden in 1980 with a critical review entitled *Sweden: The middle way on trial*. The book did not sell as well as its predecessor, but it in-

---

[77] Östberg, Kjell, "Was Sweden Headed Toward Socialism in the 1970s?," *Jacobin*, 25-08-2019.

[78] A good example can be found in a small book published by the Swedish Radio's public affairs department entitled *Har Sverige en chans? En bok från radions samhällsredaktion om krisen i västekonomierna* (Stockholm: Sveriges radio, 1978).

dicates how the US book market assessed Sweden's international reputation.[79]

A few years later, Gösta Grassman, then serving as a press officer at the Ministry of Foreign Affairs, was tasked with analysing the burgeoning trend of more critical international coverage of Sweden, particularly notable in West Germany and the United States. Grassman assessed that this critical genre lacked substantial content. The most tangible critiques focused on allegations of Swedish racism towards immigrants and minorities, alongside ongoing instances of social distress, despite the nation's advanced welfare state. Moreover, a recurring theme suggested that the Swedish welfare state masked a form of "stealth socialism," characterized by paternalism, bureaucratic rigidity, and heavy taxation. Notably, the Swedish childcare system's practice of placing children of "unsuitable" parents into foster care garnered significant attention in Western Europe, dubbed the "Kinder-Gulag" scandal in West Germany, more so than in the United States. Grassman argued that one reason why this "1984 reporting" captivated international media interest followed from its portrayal of a previously celebrated Western society as covertly totalitarian and veering towards a state socialist direction, regardless of the ruling party's ideology. Grassman refrained from pinpointing the origins of this emerging narrative within Sweden's portrayal. Retrospectively, it's challenging to ascertain whether this narrative was part of a wider campaign by an external entity. This theme resonated with the global societal pessimism post the second oil crisis, Middle Eastern unrest, computerization anxieties, and the onset of the so-called second Cold War between Reagan's USA and Brezhnev's USSR, marked by a palpable fear of Soviet influence in the West. Simultaneously, it mirrored a significant dip in Swedish public debate's self-confidence, mingling worries of economic lag with doubts about the Swedish social model's longevity. The shock value of this "1984 theme" was no

[79] Childs, Marquis W., *Sweden: The middle way on trial* (New Haven: Yale Univ. Press, 1980).

less profound domestically, as it was prominently featured in Swedish press and public discourse during the era.[80]

Reflecting on this with the benefit of hindsight reveals a paradox: the Swedish economy did not fall behind its Western counterparts to any significant degree; in fact, it fared somewhat better. Yet, contemporary discourse did not reflect this reality, with many commentators highlighting the rapid ascent of Asia's tiger economies as Sweden's principal competition. Despite this, Swedish public diplomacy efforts in the United States during this period were evidently effective: Scandinavian cultural events made their rounds across American cities, and the bicentennial celebration of diplomatic ties between Sweden and the US culminated in President Reagan – perhaps unexpectedly given his reputation – proclaiming April 4, 1983, as "Swedish-American Friendship Day." Obviously, a more critical portrayal of Sweden in the US media did not necessarily indicate a profound or reciprocal strain on Swedish-American relations.[81]

But in Stockholm, the issue was taken very seriously. The Ministry of Foreign Affairs decided to invite the approximately 150 Stockholm-based correspondents for the international press to a press conference to encourage more nuanced reporting. The effect was the opposite. The atmosphere became even more charged when Carl Lidbom, Sweden's ambassador to Paris at the time and a former trade minister, penned an open letter in the media chastising Swedish author and philosopher Lars Gustafsson, then a professor at the University of Texas at Austin, who had shown sympathy for the foreign critique.

---

[80] Both *Expressen* and *Svenska Dagbladet* ran special features on the demise of the Swedish model, while *Dagens Nyheter* hosted a high-profile debate on the question "Is Sweden totalitarian?" in the summer and fall of 1982. Here, foreign and, not least, American ideas appeared as a kind of sounding board for Swedish self-reflection. Frenander, Anders, *Debattens vågor: Om politisk-ideologiska frågor i efterkrigstidens svenska kulturdebatt* (Göteborg: Institutionen för idé- och lärdomshistoria, Univ., 1998).

[81] See discussion in Marklund, Carl, "From 'False' Neutrality to 'True' Socialism: Unofficial US 'Sweden-bashing' During the Later Palme Years, 1973–1986," *Journal of Transnational American Studies*, Vol. 7, No. 1 (2016), 1–18.

This episode drew significant attention from the American media, with correspondents in Stockholm taking heed. The French press showed even keener interest, partly because the incident involved the high-profile Parisian ambassador and partly because Gustafsson was portrayed as a sort of Swedish dissident or intellectual in exile, voicing truths critical of the establishment.

However, as the domestic editorial pages erupted in debate over Sweden's international image, Wilhelm Wachtmeister, Sweden's ambassador to Washington, felt compelled to highlight that Sweden generally received positive coverage in the United States. He observed that the most frequent complaint from Americans, encompassing both journalists and tourists, was about the taxi queues at Arlanda Airport. This comment, while shedding light on a specific aspect of American visitors' experiences, likely painted an overly simplistic picture of American public opinion at the time, considering it pertained only to those who had recently visited Sweden – a relatively small demographic.[82]

The coexistence of such starkly contrasting evaluations might seem surprising at first glance. However, most societies harbour inherent paradoxes and contradictions. Specifically, regarding the 1984 narratives, the contradictions appeared to be interdependent, at least as suggested by press excerpts from that period. The juxtaposition of Sweden's traditionally positive, historically rooted image against the concerning contemporary issues within the country – such as racism, social distress, the rise of computerization, and bureaucratic expansion – mirrored broader global and particularly American societal challenges. These issues, while also prevalent in other societies, perhaps even more acutely than in Sweden, served as focal points for media fascination. The critical coverage underscored the prevailing societal perceptions of the era, aligning closely with both the domestic Swedish discourse and the country's portrayal internationally.

---

[82] Marklund, Carl, "From 'False' Neutrality to 'True' Socialism: Unofficial US 'Sweden-bashing' During the Later Palme Years, 1973–1986," *Journal of Transnational American Studies*, Vol. 7, No. 1 (2016), 1–18.

This period marked Sweden's nuanced portrayal in American socio-political discussions, encapsulating a transition from being seen as an exemplary "model country" to a cautionary "monster country," to use historian of ideas Conny Mithander's vivid metaphor.[83] Nonetheless, it is crucial to recognize that these divergent perspectives coexisted, thus intricately presupposing and amplifying each other in a complex interplay. This led to a somewhat skewed and paradoxical phenomenon where Swedish problems were often amplified and depicted as uniquely severe or distinctly Swedish, perhaps more so than they truly were. This trend was accompanied by the critique against a tendency the critics identified in Swedish political culture as an ambition to pursue political remedies for nearly all forms of societal issues. Furthermore, it is a well-documented phenomenon that negative news tends to dominate storytelling and news cycles, especially when it deviates from a narrative of success. This dynamic can be understood as a form of "utopian trap,"[84] whereby the very aspiration for improving a given society may highlight and magnify its shortcomings.[85]

---

[83] Mithander, Conny, "Från mönsterland till monsterland. Folkhemska berättelser," Åke Bergvall et al. (eds.), *Berättelser i förvandling – berättande i ett intermedialt och tvärvetenskapligt perspektiv* (Karlstad: Karlstad University Studies, 2002), 53–85.

[84] Marklund, Carl, "The Utopian trap: Between contested Swedish models and benign Nordic branding," Haldor Byrkjeflot, Lars Mjøset, Mads Mordhorst & Klaus Petersen (eds.), *The making and circulation of Nordic Models, ideals and images* (Abingdon, Oxon: Routledge, 2022), 62–82.

[85] Almqvist, Kurt & Kay Glans (eds.), *Den svenska framgångssagan?* (Stockholm: Fischer & Co, 2001).

Crisis and recovery – back to the future

The assassination of Prime Minister Olof Palme in February 1986 thrust Sweden into an unprecedented global media focus. This tragic event in modern Swedish history was perceived by contemporaries as a pivotal moment that redefined Swedish society, signalling the end of an era. Palme was not only an internationally recognized political figure; his murder shattered the perception of Sweden as an exceptionally peaceful and secure society. In early March 1986, over a thousand journalists converged on Stockholm to report on Palme, the investigation into his murder, the funeral proceedings, and the Swedish societal response to the tragedy. Following this event, Sweden's portrayal shifted away from utopian or dystopian extremes, positioning it as a nation grappling with social and economic challenges akin to those faced by other countries.

The Palme assassination, along with subsequent scandals like the Bofors arms export controversy, eroded Sweden's standing as a moral exemplar. However, American media coverage primarily reflected Swedish anticipations of future developments rather than indicating a significant shift in Sweden's image in the US. Nonetheless, Sweden continued to be recognized as a quintessential welfare state, drawing keen interest from American neoliberal and neoconservative think tanks throughout the 1980s. These developments were viewed with concern in Sweden, leading to perceptions of a volatile and endangered national image abroad. In response, an initiative was launched to reassess Sweden's international informational strategy,[86] reviving the collaboration between the business sector and government that had characterized Swedish promotional efforts in the 1960s in the US and beyond. This partnership was rejuvenated, with even greater business leadership, during the relaunch of Sweden in the US to mark the 350th anniversary of the New Sweden colony in 1988. The campaign highlighted Swedish innovation and high technology, as well as traditional cultural elements like folk dancing and Dala horses, following a comprehensive review of Sweden's image in the United States. This effort was a deliberate attempt to dispel the "Swedish socialism" label, aiming to attract American investment and broaden opportunities for Swedish businesses in the US market.[87]

The centre-right electoral win in the 1991 Swedish parliamentary elections captured global attention. Analysts in the United States suggested that a wider segment of the Swedish electorate had grown disillusioned with their national model, still often labelled internationally as "socialist." The scholarly debate concerning the possibly socialist character of the Swedish model had evolved into a distinct area of academic study. However, as communism began to decline in the ideological battle of the Cold War, Sweden's appeal as a moderate option between capitalism and communism diminished, as the latter ceased to be a viable alternative. A yet more decisive factor for the "normalization" of Sweden's image was the economic crisis of the 1990s and its impact on the Swedish economy, a development that was prominently acknowledged in the evaluation of Sweden's inter-

[86] SOU 1987:49 Utredningen om de statliga insatserna inom Sverigeinformation och kulturutbytet med utlandet, *Sverigebilder: 17 svenskar ser på Sverige* (Stockholm: Allmänna förl., 1987).

[87] Marklund, Carl, "Swedishness on Stage: The New Sweden '88 Jubilee and the Renegotiations of Swedish Self-Identity," *Culture Unbound,* Vol. 13, No. 1 (2021), 66–89; see also Hellenes, Andreas Mørkved, "Positive Sweden: National Self-Help and the Struggle for a New Sweden Image," Jenny Andersson, Nikolas Glover, Orsi Husz & David Larsson Heidenblad (eds.), *Marknadens tid: Mellan folkhemskapitalism och nyliberalism* (Lund: Nordic Academic Press, 2023), 105–123.

national information efforts during the pivotal year of 1993.[88] Until that point, Sweden's GDP had been a frontrunner in the prosperity index, but during the financial crisis of the early 1990s it receded for three consecutive years. The international community's positive attention shifted from Sweden – and Finland – towards the other Nordic countries which did not experience as serious economic problems at the time. The Swedish model was still frequently cited but the citations increasingly concerned forecasts of its allegedly impending "demise." Throughout the 1990s, Sweden also faced intensified scrutiny for its sterilization policies during the interwar period and its cooperation with Nazi Germany during World War II. However, it is plausible that this criticism had a more profound effect on Sweden's self-perception than on its international reputation.[89]

Simultaneously, many of the established themes in Sweden's image not only persisted but were also amplified: Swedish products and designs continued to be recognized for their high quality, while Swedish environmental consciousness and advances in gender equality were still heralded as global exemplars. The incoming centre-right government eagerly championed Swedish democracy, gender equality, and the market economy as viable models for the newly independent Baltic States, efforts that received explicit endorsement from Washington. Swedish corporations like Ikea and Volvo not only sustained but also enhanced their brand reputations, with the Swedish heritage being marketed even more prominently as a valuable attribute. This revival mirrored the 1930s, with Sweden's image once again focused on resilience and reformative capability.

Sweden's economic resurgence post the 1990s crisis is undeniable, significantly buoyed by the Swedish IT boom, which largely benefited from the swift adoption of American technology. Yet, perspectives on the reasons, costs, and results of this recovery

[88] Ds 1993:72 Utrikesdepartementet, *Svenska bilder: Översyn av Sverigeinformationen* (Stockholm: Utrikesdep., 1993).

[89] Broberg, Gunnar & Mattias Tydén, "När svensk historia blev en världsnyhet: Steriliseringspolitiken och medierna," *Tvärsnitt. Humanistic and Social Science Research*, Vol. 20, No. 3 (1998), 2–15.

remain split. This division is mirrored in Sweden's image, especially within American politics. On one side, the "Nordic Way" has gained traction among neoliberal think tanks on the US East Coast and pro-market publications globally, including *The Economist* in the UK. Swedish administrations, irrespective of their political leanings, have been viewed as exemplars of how deregulation, privatization, and marketization could streamline one of the world's most comprehensive welfare states and thereby, purportedly, "rescue" it. This reflects a significant evolution in Sweden's portrayal over the last three decades. Conversely, figures on the American left – such as Bernie Sanders, Alexandria Ocasio-Cortez, and Bhaskar Sunkara – continue today to cite Swedish labour market policies as a paradigm, although it is evident that this often involves an idealization of Sweden of the past and an admixture of generic Nordic traits in terms of social policy.[90] As the American left commends Sweden (among other European nations), conservative commentators like Bill O'Reilly and Tucker Carlson tend to resurrect the outdated narrative of Sweden as "socialist," despite how disconnected this portrayal may be from the current realities of Swedish society. Concurrently, Sweden has become emblematic of "political correctness" – a term notorious for its lack of precision – within radical conservative circles globally.[91] Swedish policy commitments to multiculturalism, equality, and LGBTQIA+ rights and opportunities often receive positive acknowledgment in diverse international platforms and are lauded as exemplary by global civil society organizations. However, these values also encounter criticism abroad. In this context, the Nordic neighbours hold a significant position, as

[90] For example, Sunkara devotes much attention to an "idealized Sweden" in his book *The socialist manifesto: The case for radical politics in an era of extreme inequality* (London: Verso, 2019); see also discussion in Östberg, Kjell, *The Rise and Fall of Swedish Social Democracy* (London: Verso, forthcoming).

[91] Ullén, Magnus, "Political Correctness in Sweden: A Borderland Conceptual History," Dag Blanck & Adam Hjortén (eds.), *Swedish-American borderlands: New histories of transatlantic relations* (Minneapolis: University of Minnesota Press, 2021), 277–292.

these countries, despite sharing relatively similar values, welfare policies, social systems, and rights legislation, do not appear to be as distinctly recognized in these domains as Sweden.[92] The narrative surrounding Swedish political correctness, prominently disseminated by Russian state media to international audiences, notably influenced American public opinion, particularly leading up to and during President Trump's tenure and the Swedish election in 2018.[93] Intriguingly, these divergent perspectives on Sweden's image appear to reinforce its reputation as a bastion of progressivism. Over the past decade, it has become increasingly evident that "Sweden" is often symbolically coupled with progressive ideals,[94] a notion that has also resonated within the recent domestic discourse on "Swedish values."[95]

How is it that Sweden is depicted both as a laboratory for neoliberal experiments and as a paragon of political correctness? One potential explanation might be the influence of social media as a prevalent source of news, which complicates the notion of a singular, coherent image of Sweden both in the United States and elsewhere. In today's fragmented media environment, social media platforms and targeted news coverage – occasionally marked by foreign influence campaigns – play a pivotal role in shaping the perceptions of diverse demographic groups. Within these narratives, a complex tapestry of issues and dynamics emerges, where domestic politics blend with international stan-

---

[92] Edenborg, Emil, "Disinformation and gendered boundarymaking: Nordic media audiences making sense of 'Swedish decline,'" *Cooperation and Conflict*, Vol. 57, No. 4 (2022), 496–515.

[93] Colliver, Chloe, Peter Pomerantsev, Anne Applebaum & Jonathan Birdwell, *Smearing Sweden: International influence campaigns in the 2018 Swedish election* (London: ISD Global, 2018).

[94] Marklund, Carl, "Open Skies, Open Minds? Shifting Concepts of Communication and Information in Swedish Public Debate," Norbert Götz & Carl Marklund (eds.), *The Paradox of Openness: Transparency and Participation in Nordic Cultures of Consensus* (Leiden: Brill Academic Publishers, 2014), 143–172.

[95] Petersson, Olof, "Svenska värderingar som politiskt projekt." Paper presented at the Swedish Historians' Meeting, Mid Sweden University, Sundsvall, May 11, 2017.

ces, fact intertwines with fiction, and extreme viewpoints often overshadow more nuanced perspectives.

For instance, Sweden garnered significant attention in American media in the fall of 2015, when it, alongside Germany, accepted a notably large number of refugees from war-torn Syria, a period coinciding with Trump's presidential campaign, which adopted a stringent stance on immigration to the United States. This period also marked a zenith in Swedish engagement with its international image.[96] This period also marked the beginning of heightened attention from radical conservative circles towards Sweden.[97] The international media linked the Swedish government's stance to the country's long-standing reputation as progressive and humane, a legacy dating back to the end of World War II. However, this perspective was met with scepticism by the global alt-right social media community. Consequently, Sweden once again found itself contested in American public debate, serving as a cautionary tale for the right and a beacon for the left. This backdrop is essential for understanding President Trump's reference to "last night in Sweden" in early 2017. Trump alluded to Sweden's crime rates, citing a pre-recorded TV segment from Malmö, while also expressing astonishment that such issues could arise in Sweden, presumably as it is well-known for its peaceful welfare state. This indicates that, even among critics like Trump, the foundational view of Sweden as a stable welfare society persisted. The element of shock was leveraged, signifying that the statement was crafted to evoke surprise and concern.

---

[96] This interest can be seen in the recurring initiatives on the subject by Utbildningsradion. See, for example, Sveriges utbildningsradio, UR Samtiden – Bilden av Sverige i utlandet (Utbildningsradion, 2017); Sveriges utbildningsradio, UR Samtiden – Sverigebilder till Trump (Utbildningsradion, 2017); Sveriges utbildningsradio, UR Samtiden – Syrien, sexualitet och Sverigebilder (Utbildningsradion, 2019).

[97] See for example Samuel Merrill's ongoing research within the framework of the research project "The Radicalisation of Sweden's Image: A study of how radical right groups in other countries depict Sweden online" (funded by the Swedish Research Council 2022–2025).

Moreover, the clear-cut distinctions become blurred considering that the American right has commended Sweden's COVID-19 strategy, while the left and centre have shown greater scepticism – a stance that contrasts with the Swedish domestic debate.[98]

[98] Aucante, Yohann, *The Swedish experiment: The COVID-19 response and its controversies* (Bristol: Bristol University Press, 2022).

Conclusion

It is evident that contemporary political polarization has led to Sweden and various aspects of Swedish social life being utilized in diverse ways for a multitude of often contrasting purposes abroad. However, historical evidence also indicates that the image of Sweden internationally has consistently mirrored the complexities inherent in its society and has been manipulated for political ends across different epochs. A wide spectrum of experiences has been portrayed, resulting in a blend of positive and negative impressions. As most nations, Sweden has had its allies and adversaries, its proponents and detractors, both historically and in the present day. It would be too simplistic to categorize the international perception of Sweden into a dichotomy of a "good Sweden" revered by "Swedophiles" and a "bad Sweden" despised by "Swedophobes."[99] The contestation surrounding the image of Sweden can thus be interpreted as a struggle over reality, as aptly captured by the title of an anthology addressing this subject.[100]

It might appear intuitive to assume that Sweden's image abroad simply mirrors the state of affairs in this country, leading to the conclusion that Sweden's image is positive when Sweden is thriving. Historically, however, negative news from Sweden often garners heightened attention as it contrasts with the prevailing positive image of the country. Media studies have revealed that negative attention and positive perception can frequently coexist and sometimes even reinforce each other. In marketing discussions, the concept of "brand promise" is frequently associated

[99] Rapacioli, Paul, *Good Sweden, bad Sweden: The use and abuse of Swedish values in a post-truth world* (Stockholm: Volante, 2018).

[100] Truedson, Lars (Ed.), *Sverigebilden: Om journalistik och verklighet* (Stockholm: Institutet för mediestudier, 2018).

with "brand delivery." Given that Sweden's "nation brand" consistently ranks high, it is unsurprising that there is a heightened interest in scrutinizing and questioning the brand's ability to meet the expectations. Nonetheless, despite recurring crises, Sweden's generally positive image has remained intact, at least according to the latest surveys.

The connection between Sweden's image and the state of affairs in this country is thus not straightforward. An essential mechanism at play here appears to be the symbolic value attributed to purportedly Swedish values and the perception of Swedish society, both domestically and internationally. Over the period under examination, there has been a notable shift from broad values associated with tangible societal progress – such as Sweden being modern and prosperous due to its pragmatic consensus-driven approach – to more specific values tied to specific ideals, such as Sweden serving as a model for progressively oriented policies.

This shift can be understood as a transition from highlighting Swedish accomplishments to emphasizing Swedish principles. However, principles that fail to manifest as tangible social change and improved conditions become mere rhetoric. From this standpoint, critically examining Sweden's image in relation to its reality is a natural and constructive aspect of the increasingly global conversation about good societies and socially sustainable development, provided that the discourse is grounded in facts rather than misinformation.

Broadly speaking, the Sweden-related themes that capture attention remain largely consistent over time, appealing to both critics and supporters alike. It is primarily the interpretation and assessment of the underlying facts that sets them apart. These interpretations typically stem from ideologically driven motivations, where the association between Sweden and a set of values related to modernity, progressivism, and humanity throughout the past century plays a pivotal role in shaping the perception of Sweden and how it has been exploited for various purposes over time. The enduring international interest in Sweden during the study period can be attributed to its longstanding symbolic status as a bastion of equality, solidarity, and prosperity in the welfare society realm. As observed earlier, this perception has largely persisted despite instances where Swedish society, both domestically and abroad, has been perceived as falling short of these ideals. In conclusion, Sweden becomes intriguing and relevant when it challenges preconceived notions, deviating from expectations, and conversely, when it appears to confirm ideological principles, particularly concerning positive or negative aspects of the welfare state.

The study underscores the significance of the asymmetry between a large, well-known country of global relevance and a smaller, lesser-known society. In the case of smaller states, a multitude of issues and phenomena can be readily integrated into the broader societal narrative. Conversely, in the case of larger states with substantial international prominence and scrutiny, the connection between individual phenomena and the overall societal image appears more distant. Brands like Ikea, H&M, or Spotify effortlessly epitomize "Sweden," and vice versa, whereas companies like Apple, Microsoft, or Amazon seldom become synonymous with the "US" due to their global reach alongside other well-known American corporations.

From a historical standpoint, it's evident that discussions abroad rarely encompass the entirety of Sweden, a fact often overlooked when domestic discourse simplifies the international conversation under the singular label of "the Sweden image" (*Sverigebilden*). Usually, various aspects of Sweden are spotlighted on different occasions by diverse actors with distinct interests and objectives. It is remarkable how individual occurrences, marginal phenomena and arbitrary events can occasionally acquire disproportionate significance in shaping the international interest in Sweden. Over time, they may either fade into obscurity or endure to produce a lasting influence on the composite image of Sweden abroad for a prolonged period. The interplay between sudden attention to specific episodes and phenomena in Swedish social life and the enduring foundational perception of Sweden appears to be pivotal. A comparison of the primary themes throughout the period under review reveals that it is during moments of shifting narratives about Sweden that interest in the country is piqued, sparking debates about its society. Examining these shifts over the long term is particularly rewarding.

One of the aspects which made Sweden (and the other Nordic countries) internationally appealing in the 1930s was the perception of Sweden as untroubled, pragmatic, and devoid of the divisive ideological conflicts that obstructed democratic political debate and cooperation in other nations. The ethos of consensus was robust in Sweden, rooted in a recognition of the deep-seated social issues that clamoured for broad attention. Overseas, virtually all observers concurred that Swedish society seemed "good" in some sense, appearing to be largely devoid of social problems. This perception of Sweden persists in certain regions of the world, notably in Latin America, while in other parts of the world, such as the United States, the image of Sweden has become more polarized over time. Alongside the relatively benign and uncontroversial perception, a more politicized image has emerged, addressing issues such as multiculturalism, crime, gender equality, and other topics central to the ongoing cultural debate. These contradictory perceptions may even presuppose each other, as evidenced by Trump's 2017 comment.[101]

The welfare state continues to hold a central position in the image of Sweden in the United States, albeit with a shifting role. During the 1980s, much of the criticism directed towards Sweden stemmed from right-wing perspectives, advocating the dismantling of the national welfare state in favour of free enterprise, international capitalism, and conservative values. Contrastingly, in the 2010s, conservative critique shifted towards multiculturalism and immigration as perceived threats to national cohesion, both in Sweden and the United States. While the welfare state typically does not emerge as a point of defence in American radical conservative discourse, this American narrative of a

[101] Svenska Institutet, *Bilden av Sverige i Amerika – rapport från Svenska institutet 2019:2* (Stockholm: Svenska Institutet, 2019).

transformed Sweden can be aligned with the radical conservative nostalgia of a bygone America.[102]

Similarly, it is intriguing to observe how Sweden today is utilized by opposed groups for communicating highly diverse political messages. For example, US neoliberal think tanks and publications often showcase Sweden (along with other Nordic nations) as exemplars of market adaptation and innovation, highlighting their private healthcare and education sectors, among other factors. Conversely, radical conservative commentators tend to portray Swedish society as left-leaning, progressive, or "politically correct" in a broader sense, considering these attributes pivotal in shaping Swedish labour laws, welfare programs, gender equality initiatives, environmental policies, multiculturalism, and refugee reception. Meanwhile, US progressives may commend Sweden for precisely these policies, while turning a critical eye to the privatization or neoliberalization they detect in Swedish society and political economy at large. It is conceivable that these seemingly incompatible elements coexist within contemporary Sweden and in a sense this complexity is also reflected in contemporary Swedish political debate, domestically. Moreover, this conundrum is reminiscent of the fascination international observers experienced during the peak of the Swedish model in the 1970s and 1980s, marvelling at the seemingly surprising coexistence of a free-market economy alongside a comprehensive, tax-financed welfare state. Complicating matters further is the fact that both the right and the left in the United States and elsewhere tend to reference selectively different aspects of Swedish reality to bolster the punch of their arguments in the policy debates they are engaged with. As mentioned above, neoliberal think tanks have lauded Sweden as a beacon of success since the market-oriented reforms of the 1990s and beyond. However, this does not preclude the American left from con-

---

[102] Marklund, Carl, "Shifts in 'Sweden-bashing:' Themes and tropes in the critical discourse on Sweden –comparing the 1980s and the 2010s," Paper presented at the Second Nordic Challenges Conference: Narratives of uniformity and diversity, University of Helsinki, March 7–9, 2018.

tinuing to cite, for instance, the Swedish labour market and healthcare systems as potential models, often with a focus on the other Nordic countries that have not undergone similarly extensive market-friendly welfare system reforms as Sweden. Moreover, the complexity is heightened by the multi-layered nature of image-making, occurring across various levels and encompassing a myriad of issues simultaneously. For instance, during the Covid-19 pandemic, American right-wing extremists could simultaneously criticize Sweden for its purported multiculturalism while applauding its perceived "liberal" approach to managing the pandemic. In terms of political rhetoric, "Sweden" is rarely used as a total image, but as a palette of various policies and phenomena that may be assembled in varying ways depending upon the proclivities and needs of the beholder.

In today's globalized media landscape, the ubiquity of social media has facilitated the rapid dissemination of false or distorted messages, particularly by influential individuals, regardless of their veracity. However, this phenomenon is not new, as exemplified by the episode of Eisenhower's infamous suicide statement. The significance of individual texts authored by figures such as Childs, Brown, Servan-Schreiber, and Huntford – each with their own agendas – cannot be overstated in shaping the historical image of Sweden. These historical actors often presented comprehensive narratives about the whole of Sweden, contributing in various ways to the enduring images of Sweden that circulate today. Contrastingly, in today's fragmented and global media landscape, individual statements and events – mere fragments or shards of the kaleidoscopic reality that diverges significantly from the daily experiences of contemporary Sweden – appear to have the greatest momentary impact but perhaps also a shorter lifespan in public consciousness.

From the standpoint of nation branding, public diplomacy, and official informational efforts, it is noteworthy that endeavours to counter inaccuracies, correct exaggerations, and "polish" the discourse surrounding Sweden to nurture its image have historically encountered limited success, at least if judged by the evidenced provided by American sources. Conversely, from the Swedish perspective, greater success has been achieved when official representatives of Sweden have opted to acknowledge and adapt possibly critical themes in foreign perceptions of Sweden but reinterpret them in alignment with more positive values, as demonstrated by the case of the "Swedish sin" in the 1960s. However, this approach is not without controversy, as certain segments of Swedish public opinion, such as religious groups, opponents of pornography, and conservatives, have continuously contested such associations and it is likely that official information efforts will remain sensitive also in the future.

Over the years, it has been crucial for Swedish representatives – including diplomats, politicians, trade unions, and the business community – to navigate differing interpretations of the Swedish social model. This complexity was particularly evident during the polarized 1960s when "Swedish socialism" gained widespread usage, initially garnering positive interest from the international political left and radical social scientists. However, it gradually came to be perceived as a departure from the free-market principles by prominent figures on the global political right and international economists. The Swedish charm offensive during the New Sweden anniversary in the United States in 1988 exemplifies a deliberate effort by the Swedish business community to refine the image of Sweden, particularly in the American industrial and financial sectors they sought to engage, by downplaying the "socialist" element in its foreign perception. This occurred amidst a domestic political battle concerning "fund socialism" in the aftermath of the wage earner funds controversy.

Sweden's relationship with foreign powers has naturally been a decisive factor for the perception of the country abroad but it is not self-evident how these relations impact upon perceptions. Drawing parallels, for instance, between the criticism of the US involvement in the Vietnam War and the support for North Vietnam, including American deserters in the early 1970s, and the contemporary critique of the democratic trajectory of countries like Russia, Hungary, and Turkey, coupled with Turkey's stance towards the Kurds, underscores the impact of such tensions on Sweden's image. Studies indicate that countries perceiving themselves as criticized by Sweden experience shifts in their perception of the country, while opinion polls conducted during the "years of frost" in the 1970s in the United States suggest minimal impact. Although the reliability of later studies may be questioned, it is reasonable to assume that media played a pivotal role. Unlike the Turkish and Russian governments today, the US administration had limited ability to influence press coverage of Sweden.

This raises the question of the extent to which various influence campaigns have shaped Sweden's image, both historically and presently. Historically, most attempts to utilize images of Sweden during the studied period have had minimal impact on influencing Swedish society's development. However, the exaggerated portrayal and factual inaccuracies surrounding topics like "Swedish sin" and suicide statistics in the US during the 1960s, which reinforced conservative and religious opinions, highlight a different scenario. Similarly, the persistent focus on the Swedish social model and "high tax policy" by American neoliberal think tanks in the 1980s primarily stemmed from professional interest rather than illegitimate attempts at influence. Regarding instances such as the Kinder-Gulag, which could be considered an early parallel to today's LVU campaign,[103] the Swedish Foreign Ministry responded by questioning the origin and sought to directly intervene to correct the perception of foreign media. In retrospect, it is challenging to determine the extent to which the American perceptions under examination were entirely spontaneous or influenced, in part, by Swedish information campaigns or deliberate actions. But historically direct attempts to rectify fake news and alternative facts have rather tended to cement the narratives they were designed to refute.

---

[103] Ranstorp, Magnus & Linda Ahlerup, *LVU-kampanjen: Desinformation, konspirationsteorier, och kopplingarna mellan det inhemska och det internationella i relation till informationspåverkan från icke-statliga aktörer* (Stockholm: Försvarshögskolan, Centrum för totalförsvar och samhällets säkerhet, 2023).

After reviewing the fluctuations in the portrayals of Sweden, particularly in American material, it is remarkable how frequently the image of Sweden has been depicted as being in crisis while the country has been simultaneously portrayed as a fundamentally progressive society striving to address complex social issues. This dual portrayal mirrors the international attention given to the "Nordic model."[104] Sweden has, in a sense, been both idealized and devalued, borrowing the terminology of cultural geographer Madeleine Eriksson, who described similar mechanisms shaping the construction of the "Norrland image" in the Swedish public sphere during the same period.[105]

As mentioned earlier, it is inaccurate to characterize Sweden's image as singular, whether historically or presently. For instance, during the "years of frost" in the 1970s, official Swedish-American relations experienced significant strain at the highest political and diplomatic levels, yet this tension did not notably impact American public opinion, nor did it hinder exchanges between the two countries at other levels. Even during the 1980s, when Sweden and the United States found common ground in various areas, Sweden's image was tarnished to an even greater extent. In democratic relationships where the state does not exert full control over all societal functions, it's noteworthy that different groups tend to harbour distinct perceptions based on their professional interests – be it military, academic, commercial, technological, or cultural – thereby contributing to the diverse array of images of Sweden in the US. Furthermore, these perceptions often intersect, even when they appear contradictory.

Like any concept of society, the image of Sweden – both domestically and internationally – is inherently political, thus

[104] Koivunen, Anu, Jari Ojala & Janne Holmén, "Always in crisis, always a solution? The Nordic model as a political and scholarly concept," Anu Koivunen, Jari Ojala & Janne Holmén (eds.), *The Nordic economic, social and political model: Challenges in the 21st century* (London: Routledge, 2021), 1–19.

[105] Eriksson, Madeleine, *(Re)producing a periphery: Popular representations of the Swedish North* (Umeå: Department of Cultural Geography, Umeå University, 2010).

rendering it controversial. The portrayal of Sweden has frequently been scrutinized because it has been predominantly positive yet concurrently problematic, allowing for diverse interpretations and uses over time. However, this division, both abroad and domestically, appears more pronounced today. Evidently, the dissemination of Sweden's image intensifies in contexts and situations where it can be politicized, where it can be used by actors for their purposes. When Sweden's image becomes imbued with political significance and utilized for political ends it gains heightened relevance. The interplay between complementary and conflicting images of Sweden and Swedish society engenders cognitive dissonance and fundamental paradoxes, fuelling ongoing curiosity and intrigue.

References

Alm, Martin, *Americanitis: Amerika som sjukdom eller läkemedel: Svenska berättelser om USA åren 1900–1939* (Lund: Nordic Academic Press, 2002).

Almqvist, Kurt & Kay Glans (eds.), *Den svenska framgångssagan?* (Stockholm: Fischer & Co, 2001).

Andersson, Jenny, *Between growth and security: Swedish social democracy from a strong society to a third way* (Manchester: Manchester university press, 2006).

Andersson, Jenny, "Nordic Nostalgia and Nordic Light: The Swedish model as Utopia 1930–2007," *Scandinavian Journal of History*, Vol. 34, No. 3 (2009), 229–245.

Andersson, Jenny & Mary Hilson, "Images of Sweden and the Nordic Countries," *Scandinavian Journal of History*, Vol. 34, No. 3 (2009), 219–228.

Andrén, Nils & Yngve Möller, *Från Undén till Palme: Svensk utrikespolitik efter andra världskriget* (Stockholm: Norstedt, 1990).

Arnberg, Klara, "Capital of sex: Pornography sales in Stockholm, 1965–1985," *Porn Studies*, Vol. 9, No. 1 (2021), 56–81.

Aronczyk, Melissa, *Branding the nation: The global business of national identity* (Oxford: Oxford University Press, 2013).

Aucante, Yohann, *The Swedish experiment: The COVID-19 response and its controversies* (Bristol: Bristol University Press, 2022).

Bengtsson, Erik, *Världens jämlikaste land?* (Lund: Arkiv förlag, 2020).

Biltekin, Nevra, Leos Müller & Magnus Petersson (eds.), *200 years of peace: New perspectives on modern Swedish foreign policy* (New York: Berghahn, 2022).

Björklund, Elisabet & Mariah Larsson (eds.), *Swedish cinema and the sexual revolution: Critical essays* (Jefferson, North Carolina: McFarland, 2016).

Blanck, Dag & Adam Hjorthén (eds.), *Swedish-American borderlands: New histories of transatlantic relations* (Minneapolis: University of Minnesota Press, 2021).

Broberg, Gunnar & Mattias Tydén, "När svensk historia blev en världsnyhet: Steriliseringspolitiken och medierna," *Tvärsnitt. Humanistisk och samhällsvetenskaplig forskning*, Vol. 20, No. 3 (1998), 2–15.

Browning, Christopher, *Nation branding and international politics* (Montreal & Kingston: McGill-Queen's University Press, 2023).

Byrkjeflot, Haldor, Lars Mjøset, Mads Mordhorst & Klaus Petersen (eds.), *The making and circulation of Nordic models, ideals and images* (Abingdon, Oxon: Routledge, 2022).

Byström, Mikael & Pär Frohnert (Red.), *Reaching a state of hope: Refugees, immigrants and the Swedish welfare state, 1930–2000* (Lund: Nordic Academic Press, 2013).

Childs, Marquis W., *Sweden: The middle way* (New Haven: Yale Univ. Press, 1936).

Childs, Marquis W., *Sweden: The middle way on trial* (New Haven: Yale Univ. Press, 1980).

Clerc, Louis, Nikolas Glover & Paul Jordan (eds.), *Histories of public diplomacy and nation branding in the Nordic and Baltic countries: Representing the periphery* (Leiden: Brill, 2015).

Clerc, Louis, *Cultural diplomacy in Cold War Finland: Identity, geopolitics and the welfare state* (Cham: Palgrave Macmillan, 2023).

Colliver, Chloe, Peter Pomerantsev, Anne Applebaum & Jonathan Birdwell, *Smearing Sweden: International influence campaigns in the 2018 Swedish election* (London: ISD Global, 2018).

Ds 1993:72 Utrikesdepartementet, *Svenska bilder: Översyn av Sverigeinformationen* (Stockholm: Utrikesdep., 1993).

Edenborg, Emil, "Disinformation and gendered boundarymaking: Nordic media audiences making sense of 'Swedish decline,'" *Cooperation and Conflict*, Vol. 57, No. 4 (2022), 496–515.

Ekengren, Ann-Marie, *Olof Palme och utrikespolitiken: Europa och Tredje världen* (Umeå: Boréa, 2005).

Eriksson, Madeleine, *(Re)producing a periphery: Popular representations of the Swedish North* (Umeå: Kulturgeografiska institutionen, Umeå universitet, 2010).

Erlandsson, Johan, *Desertörerna* (Stockholm: Carlsson, 2016).

Eyerman, Ron & Andrew Jamison, *On the transatlantic migration of knowledge: Aspects of intellectual exchange between the United States and Sweden, 1930–1970* (Umeå: Cerum, 1992).

Frenander, Anders, *Debattens vågor: Om politisk-ideologiska frågor i efterkrigstidens svenska kulturdebatt* (Göteborg: Institutionen för idé- och lärdomshistoria, Univ., 1998).

Gienow-Hecht, Jessica, "Nation Branding: A Useful Category for International History," *Diplomacy & Statecraft*, Vol. 30, No. 4 (2019), 755–779.

Glover, Nikolas & Carl Marklund, "Arabian Nights in the Midnight Sun? Exploring the temporal structure of sexual geographies," *Historisk Tidskrift*, Vol. 129, No. 3 (2009), 487–510.

Glover, Nikolas, *National relations: Public diplomacy, national identity and the Swedish Institute 1945–1970* (Lund: Nordic Academic Press, 2011).

Glover, Nikolas & Andreas Mørkved Hellenes, "A 'Swedish Offensive' at the World's Fairs: Advertising, Social Reformism and the Roots of Swedish Cultural Diplomacy, 1935–1939," *Contemporary European History*, Vol. 30, No. 2 (2021), 284–300.

Habel, Ylva, *Modern media, modern audiences: Mass media and social engineering in the 1930s Swedish welfare state* (Stockholm: Aura, 2002).

Hale, Frederick, "Challenging the Swedish Social Welfare State: The Case of Dwight David Eisenhower," *Swedish-American Historical Quarterly*, Vol. 54, No. 1 (2003), 55–71.

Hale, Frederick, "'Time' for Sex in Sweden: Enhancing the Myth of the 'Swedish Sin' during the 1950s," *Scandinavian Studies*, Vol. 75, No. 3 (2003), 351–374.

Hale, Frederick, "Brave New World in Sweden? Roland Huntford's *The New Totalitarians*," *Scandinavian Studies*, Vol. 78, nr. 2 (2006), 167–190.

Hellenes, Andreas Mørkved & Carl Marklund, "Sweden Goes Global: Francophonie, Palme, and the North-South Dialogue during the Cold War," *Histoire@Politique. Politique, culture, société*, Nr. 35 (2018).

Hellenes, Andreas Mørkved, *Fabricating Sweden. Studies of Swedish public diplomacy in France from the 1930s to the 1990s*. Doctoral dissertation (Paris & Oslo: Sciences Po Paris & University of Oslo, 2019).

Hellenes, Andreas Mørkved, "Tracing the Nordic Model: French Creations, Swedish Appropriations and Nordic Articulations," Haldor Byrkjeflot, Mads Mordhorst, Lars Mjøset & Klaus Pedersen (eds.), *The making and circulation of Nordic models, ideals and images* (Abingdon, Oxon: Routledge, 2022), 83–101.

Hellenes, Andreas Mørkved, "Positiva Sverige: Nationell självhjälp och kampen för en ny Sverigebild," Jenny Andersson, Nikolas Glover, Orsi Husz & David Larsson Heidenblad (eds.), *Marknadens tid* (Lund: Nordic Academic Press, 2023), 105–123.

Hendin, Herbert, *Suicide and Scandinavia: A psychoanalytic study of culture and character* (New York: Grune & Stratton, 1964).

Hilson, Mary, "Consumer Co-operation and Economic Crisis: The 1936 Roosevelt Inquiry on Co-operative Enterprise and the Emergence of the Nordic 'Middle Way,'" *Contemporary European History*, Vol. 22, nr. 2 (2013), 181–198.

Hinshaw, David, *Sweden: Champion of peace* (New York: Putnam, 1949).

Hjorthén, Adam, *Border-crossing commemorations: Entangled histories of Swedish settling in America* (Stockholm: Department of History, Stockholm University, 2015).

Holmström, Mikael, *Den dolda alliansen: Sveriges hemliga NATO-förbindelser* (Stockholm: Atlantis, 2011).

Huntford, Roland, *The new totalitarians* (London: Allen Lane, 1971).

Jackson, Walter A., *Gunnar Myrdal and America's conscience: Social engineering and racial liberalism, 1938–1987* (Chapel Hill: University of North Carolina Press, 1990).

Jervis, Robert, *Perception and misperception in international politics* (Princeton, N.J.: Princeton U.P., 1976).

Joesten, Joachim, *Stalwart Sweden* (Garden City: Doubleday, Doran and Co., Inc., 1943).

Johansson, Martin, *De nordiska lekarna: Grannländer i pressen under olympiska vinterspel* (Huddinge: Södertörns högskola, 2023).

Kaneva, Nadia S., "Simulation Nations: Nation Brands and Baudrillard's Theory of Media," *European Journal of Cultural Studies*, Vol. 21, nr. 5 (2018), 631–648.

Kastrup, Allan, *The making of Sweden* (Stockholm: Svensk-amerikanska nyhetsbyrån & Tiden, 1953).

Kastrup, Allan, *Med Sverige i Amerika: Opinioner, stämningar och upplysningsarbete: En rapport* (Malmö: Corona, 1985).

Koivunen, Anu, Jari Ojala & Janne Holmén, "Always in crisis, always a solution? The Nordic model as a political and scholarly concept," Anu Koivunen, Jari Ojala & Janne Holmén (eds.), *The Nordic economic, social and political model: Challenges in the 21st century* (London: Routledge, 2021), 1–19.

Kuldkepp, Mart, *Estonia gravitates towards Sweden: Nordic identity and activist regionalism in World War I* (Tartu: University of Tartu Press, 2014).

Kummel, Bengt, *Svenskar i all världen förenen eder! Vilhelm Lundström och den allsvenska rörelsen* (Åbo: Åbo Akademi, 1994).

Kungliga biblioteket, Svenska dagstidningar: https://tidningar.kb.se/?q=%22sverigebilden%22&sort=asc.

Kylhammar, Martin, *Frejdiga framstegsmän och visionära världsmedborgare: Epokskiftet 20-tal–30-tal genom Fem unga och Lubbe Nordström* (Stockholm: Akademeja, 1994).

Kylhammar, Martin, *Bland resenärer och kosmopoliter: Svensk kultur inför utlandet* (Stockholm: Carlsson, 2017).

Lennerhed, Lena, *Frihet att njuta: Sexualdebatten i Sverige på 1960-talet* (Stockholm: Norstedt, 1994).

Lundberg, Jonathan, *Sverigevänner: Ett reportage om det svenska nätkriget* (Stockholm: Piratförlaget, 2020).

Lundberg, Urban & Mattias Tydén (eds.), *Sverigebilder: Det nationellas betydelser i politik och vardag* (Stockholm: Institutet för Framtidsstudier, 2008).

Lundin, Per, Niklas Stenlås & Johan Gribbe (eds.), *Science for welfare and warfare: Technology and state initiative in cold war Sweden* (Sagamore Beach: Science History Publications, 2010).

Marklund, Carl, "The Social Laboratory, the Middle Way, and the Swedish Model: Three Frames for the Image of Sweden," *Scandinavian Journal of History*, Vol. 34, No. 3 (2009), 264–285.

Marklund, Carl & Peter Stadius, "Acceptance and Conformity: Merging Nationalism with Modernity in the Stockholm Exhibition in 1930," *Culture Unbound. Journal of Current Cultural Research*, Vol. 2 (2010), 609–634.

Marklund, Carl, "Sharing values and shaping values: Sweden, 'Nordic Democracy' and the American Crisis," Jussi Kurunmäki & Johan Strang (eds.), *Rhetorics of Nordic democracy* (Helsinki: Finnish Literature Society, 2010), 114–140.

Marklund, Carl, "A Swedish *Norden* or a Nordic Sweden? Image Politics in the West during the Cold War," Jonas Harvard & Peter Stadius (eds.), *Communicating the North: Media structures and images in the making of the Nordic region* (Farnham: Ashgate, 2013), 263–287.

Marklund, Carl, "Open Skies, Open Minds? Shifting Concepts of Communication and Information in Swedish Public Debate," Norbert Götz & Carl Marklund (eds.), *The Paradox of Openness: Transparency and Participation in Nordic Cultures of Consensus* (Leiden: Brill Academic Publishers, 2014), 143–172.

Marklund, Carl, "From 'False' Neutrality to 'True' Socialism: Unofficial US 'Sweden-bashing' During the Later Palme Years, 1973–1986," *Journal of Transnational American Studies*, Vol. 7, No. 1 (2016), 1–18.

Marklund, Carl, *Neutrality and solidarity in Nordic humanitarian action* (London: Overseas Development Institute, 2016).

Marklund, Carl, "Shifts in 'Sweden-bashing:' Themes and tropes in the critical discourse on Sweden – comparing the 1980s and the 2010s," Paper presented at the Second Nordic Challenges Conference: Narratives of uniformity and diversity, Helsingfors universitet, 7–9 mars 2018.

Marklund, Carl, "Double Loyalties? Small-State Solidarity and the Debates on New International Economic Order in Sweden During the Long 1970s," *Scandinavian Journal of History*, Vol. 45, No. 3 (2019), 384–406.

Marklund, Carl, "Soft Power," Audrey Kobayashi (ed.), *International Encyclopedia of Human Geography* (Oxford: Elsevier, 2020), 291–296.

Marklund, Carl, "Swedishness on Stage: The New Sweden '88 Jubilee and the Renegotiations of Swedish Self-Identity," *Culture Unbound*, Vol. 13, No. 1 (2021), 66–89.

Marklund, Carl, "The Utopian trap: Between contested Swedish models and benign Nordic branding," Haldor Byrkjeflot, Lars Mjøset, Mads Mordhorst & Klaus Petersen (eds.), *The making and circulation of Nordic models, ideals and images* (Abingdon, Oxon: Routledge, 2022), 62–82.

Marklund, Carl, "Krångla lagom! Välfärdsstatskritiken och byråkratiseringsdebatten," Jenny Andersson, Nikolas Glover, Orsi Husz & David Larsson Heidenblad (eds.), *Marknadens tid: Mellan folkhemskapitalism och nyliberalism* (Lund: Nordic Academic Press, 2023), 33–53.

Marklund, Carl & Byron Z. Rom-Jensen, *Swedish progressivism: US debates, transatlantic circulations and Nordic models* (Abingdon, Oxon: Routledge, kommande).

Mays, Christin, *Have money, will travel: Scholarships and academic exchange between Sweden and the United States, 1912–1980* (Uppsala: Acta Universitatis Upsaliensis, 2022).

Mithander, Conny, "Från mönsterland till monsterland. Folkhemska berättelser," Åke Bergvall et al. (eds.), *Berättelser i förvandling – berättande i ett intermedialt och tvärvetenskapligt perspektiv* (Karlstad: Karlstad University Studies, 2002), 53–85.

Mjøset, Lars, "Social science, humanities, and the 'Nordic model,'" Haldor Byrkjeflot, Lars Mjøset, Mads Mordhorst & Klaus Petersen (eds.), *The making and circulation of Nordic models, ideals and images* (Abingdon, Oxon: Routledge, 2022), 34–61.

Morey, Maribel, *White philanthropy: Carnegie Corporation's* An American dilemma *and the making of a white world order* (Chapel Hill: University of North Carolina Press, 2021).

Musiał, Kazimierz, *Roots of the Scandinavian model: Images of progress in the era of modernisation* (Baden-Baden: Nomos-Verl.-Ges., 2002).

Myrdal, Alva & Gunnar Myrdal, *Kontakt med Amerika* (Stockholm: Bonnier, 1941).

Mörth, Ulrika & Bengt Sundelius, *Interdependens, konflikt och säkerhetspolitik: Sverige och den amerikanska teknikexportkontrollen* (Stockholm: Nerenius & Santérus, 1998).

Nelson, George R. (ed.), *Freedom and welfare: Social patterns in the northern countries of Europe* (Copenhagen, 1953).

Nordström, Ludvig, *Lort-Sverige* (Stockholm: Kooperativa förbundets bokförlag, 1938).

Nye, Jr., Joseph S., *Soft power: The means to success in world politics* (New York: Public Affairs, 2004)

O'Dell, Tom, *Culture unbound: Americanization and everyday life in Sweden* (Lund: Nordic Academic Press, 1997).

Ohlsson, Per T., *Over there: Banden över Atlanten* (Stockholm: Timbro, 1992).

Ottosson, Sten, *Den (o)moraliska neutraliteten: Tre politikers och tre tidningars moraliska värdering av svensk utrikespolitik 1945–1952* (Stockholm: Santérus, 2000).

Ottosson, Sten, *Sverige mellan öst och väst: Svensk självbild under kalla kriget* (Göteborg: Statsvetenskapliga institutionen, Göteborgs univ. 2001).

Pamment, James, *New public diplomacy in the 21st century: A comparative study of policy and practice* (London: Routledge, 2013).

Patel, Kiran Klaus, *The New Deal: A Global History* (Princeton: Princeton University Press, 2016).

Pehrson, Lennart, *Den nya världen*. Vols. 1–3 (Stockholm: Bonnier, 2014).

Petersson, Olof, "Svenska värderingar som politiskt projekt." Paper presented at the Swedish Historians' Meeting, Mid Sweden University, Sundsvall, May 11, 2017.

Ranstorp, Magnus & Linda Ahlerup, *LVU-kampanjen: Desinformation, konspirationsteorier, och kopplingarna mellan det inhemska och det internationella i relation till informationspåverkan från icke-statliga aktörer* (Stockholm: Försvarshögskolan, Centrum för totalförsvar och samhällets säkerhet, 2023).

Rapacioli, Paul, *Good Sweden, bad Sweden: The use and abuse of Swedish values in a post-truth world* (Stockholm: Volante, 2018).

Response Analysis Corporation, *Knowledge of and attitudes toward Sweden: Nationwide studies among the American public* (Princeton, N.J.: Response analysis corporation, 1973).

Rodgers, Daniel T., *Atlantic crossings: Social politics in a progressive age* (Cambridge, Mass.: Belknap Press of Harvard University Press, 1998).

Rom-Jensen, Byron Z., *The Scandinavian legacy: Nordic policies as images and models in the United States*. Doctoral dissertation (Aarhus: Aarhus University, 2017).

Rom-Jensen, Byron Z., "A Model of Social Security? The political usage of Scandinavia in Roosevelt's New Deal," *Scandinavian Journal of History*, Vol. 42, No. 4 (2017), 363–388.

Rom-Jensen, Byron Z., "'A cross between Batman and a public ear:' How the United States transformed the ombudsman," Haldor Byrkjeflot, Lars Mjøset, Mads Mordhorst & Klaus Petersen (eds.), *The making and circulation of Nordic models, ideals and images* (Abingdon, Oxon: Routledge, 2022), 145–164.

Rom-Jensen, Byron Z., "Enthusiastic Proselytisers: Translating the Swedish Gender Policy Model in Cold War United States," *Contemporary European History*, Vol. 31, No. 3 (2022), 401–419.

Rom-Jensen, Byron Z., Andreas Mørkved Hellenes, Mary Hilson & Carl Marklund, "Modelizing the Nordics: Transdiscursive migrations of Nordic models, c. 1965–2020," *Scandinavian Journal of History*, Vol. 48, No. 2 (2023), 249–271.

Rothstein, Bo, *Grundbulten: Tillit och visionen om en liberal socialism* (Stockholm: Fri tanke, 2023).

Ryan, Alexander, *How partisan emotions and negativity shape our politics* (Sundsvall: Mid Sweden University, 2023).

Rystad, Göran, Klaus-Richard Böhme & Wilhelm M. Carlgren (eds.), *In quest of trade and security: The Baltic in power politics 1500–1990.* Vol. 2 1890–1990 (Stockholm: Probus, 1995).

Rågsjö-Thorell, Andreas, "Storbolagen oroliga över gängvåldets effekter på Sverigebilden: 'Svårt att locka rätt kompetens,'" *Resumé*, 2023-10-20. https://www.resume.se/alla-nyheter/morgonsvepet/storbolagen-oroliga-over-gangvaldets-effekter-pa-sverigebilden-svart-att-locka-ratt-kompetens/.

Schivelbusch, Wolfgang, *Three new deals: Roosevelt's America, Mussolini's Italy, Hitler's Germany, and the rise of state power in the 1930's* (New York: Metropolitan Books, 2006).

Scott, Carl-Gustaf, *Swedish social democracy and the Vietnam War* (Huddinge: Södertörn University, 2017).

Servan-Schreiber, Jean-Jacques, *Le défi americain* (Paris: Denoël, 1967).

Silva, Charles, *Keep them strong, keep them friendly: Swedish-American relations and the Pax Americana, 1948–1952* (Stockholm: Univ., 1999).

SOU 1987:49 Utredningen om de statliga insatserna inom Sverigeinformationen och kulturutbytet med utlandet, *Sverigebilder: 17 svenskar ser på Sverige* (Stockholm: Allmänna förl., 1987).

Stadius, Peter, "Happy Countries: Appraisals of Interwar Nordic Societies," Jonas Harvard & Peter Stadius (eds.), *Communicating the North: Media structures and images in the making of the Nordic region* (Farnham: Ashgate, 2013), 241–262.

Strode, Hudson, *Sweden: Model for a world* (New York: Harcourt, Brace, 1949).

Sunkara, Bhaskar, *The socialist manifesto: The case for radical politics in an era of extreme inequality* (London: Verso, 2019).

Svenska Institutet, *Bilden av Sverige i Amerika – rapport från Svenska institutet 2019:2* (Stockholm: Svenska Institutet, 2019).

Svenska Institutet, *Bilden av Sverige utomlands 2022. Årsrapport från Svenska institutet* (Stockholm: Svenska Institutet, 2023).

Svenska Institutet, *Bilden av Sverige utomlands 2023. Årsrapport från Svenska institutet* (Stockholm: Svenska Institutet, 2024).

Svensson, Göran, "Utländska bilder av Sverige: Bespeglingar i det moderna," Ulf Himmelstrand & Göran Svensson (eds.), *Sverige – vardag och struktur: Sociologer beskriver det svenska samhället* (Stockholm: Norstedts Förlag, 1988), 139–161.

Sveriges radio. Samhällsredaktionen, *Har Sverige en chans? En bok från radions samhällsredaktion om krisen i västekonomierna* (Stockholm: Sveriges radio, 1978).

Sveriges utbildningsradio, UR Samtiden – Bilden av Sverige i utlandet (Utbildningsradion, 2017).

Sveriges utbildningsradio, UR Samtiden – Sverigebilder till Trump (Utbildningsradion, 2017).

Sveriges utbildningsradio, UR Samtiden – Syrien, sexualitet och Sverigebilder (Utbildningsradion, 2019).

Sörlin, Sverker, *Framtidslandet: Debatten om Norrland och naturresurserna under det industriella genombrottet* (Stockholm: Carlsson, 1988).

The American-Swedish News Exchange, inc., New York, *Reports on Sweden by American Newspapermen, 1949: A Scrapbook* (New York: American-Swedish News Exchange, 1949).

Thorsell, Staffan, *Sverige i Vita huset* (Stockholm: Bonnier fakta, 2004).

Tistedt, Petter, *Visioner om medborgerliga publiker: Medier och socialreformism på 1930-talet* (Höör: Brutus Östlings förlag Symposion, 2013).

Truedson, Lars (ed)., *Sverigebilden: Om journalistik och verklighet* (Stockholm: Institutet för mediestudier, 2018).

Ullén, Magnus, "Political Correctness in Sweden: A Borderland Conceptual History," Dag Blanck & Adam Hjortén (eds.), *Swedish-American borderlands: New histories of transatlantic relations* (Minneapolis: University of Minnesota Press, 2021), 277–292.

Viktorin, Carolin, Jessica Gienow-Hecht, Annika Estner & Marcel K. Will, *Branding in Modern History* (Oxford & New York: Berghahn Books, 2018).

Wallengren, Ann-Kristin, *Välkommen hem Mr Swanson: Svenska emigranter och svenskhet på film* (Lund: Nordic Academic Press, 2013).

Werner, Jeff, *Medelvägens estetik: Sverigebilder i USA*. Vols. 1 & 2 (Hedemora: Gidlund, 2008).

Westberg, Jacob, *Svenska säkerhetsstrategier: Från neutralitetspolitik till ansökan om Natomedlemskap* (Lund: Studentlitteratur, 2023).

Åkerlund, Andreas, *Public diplomacy and academic mobility in Sweden: The Swedish Institute and scholarship programs for foreign academics, 1938–2010* (Lund: Nordic Academic Press, 2016).

Åsard, Erik (Red.), *Det blågula stjärnbaneret: USA:s närvaro och inflytande i Sverige* (Stockholm: Carlsson, 2016).

Östberg, Kjell, "Was Sweden Headed Toward Socialism in the 1970s?," *Jacobin*, 2019-08-25.

Östberg, Kjell, *The Rise and Fall of Swedish Social Democracy* (London: Verso, forthcoming).

Östlund, David, *Det sociala kriget och kapitalets ansvar: Social ingenjörskonst mellan affärsintresse och samhällsreform i USA och Sverige 1899–1914* (Stockholm: Institutionen för litteraturvetenskap och idéhistoria, Univ, 2003).

Issues of Contemporary History / Samtidshistoriska frågor

The series serves as a platform for the examination of historical events and contemporary issues. It presents edited transcripts from witness seminars and oral histories, complemented by original research and conference documentation. Accessible through the link: https://bibl-app.sh.se/publicationseries/list?id=12, most titles are also available for free download via the Digital Science Archive, DiVA (http://www.diva-portal.se).

Professor Norbert Götz (norbert.gotz@sh.se) oversees the series on behalf of The Institute of Contemporary History (*Samtidshistoriska institutet*, SHI) at Södertörn University. Additionally, selected titles are the result of collaborations with the Center for Baltic and East European Studies (CBEES).

1. *Olof Palme i sin tid*. Ed. Kjell Östberg (2001).
2. *Kvinnorörelsen och '68*. Ed. Elisabeth Elgán (2001).
3. *Riv alla murar! Vittnesseminarier om sexliberalismen och om Pockettidningen R*. Ed. Lena Lennerhed (2002).
4. *Löntagarfonderna – en missad möjlighet?* Ed. Lars Ekdahl (2002).
5. *Dagens Nyheter: Minnesseminarium över Sven-Erik Larsson. Vittnesseminarium om DN och '68*. Ed. Alf W. Johansson (2003).
6. *Kvinnorna skall göra det! Den kvinnliga medborgarskolan på Fogelstad – som idé, text och historia*. Eds. Ebba Witt Brattström & Lena Lennerhed (2003).
7. *Moderaterna, marknaden och makten – svensk högerpolitik under avregleringens tid, 1976–1991*. Torbjörn Nilsson (2003).
8. *Upprorets estetik. Vittnesseminarier om kulturens politisering under 1960- och 1970-talet*. Ed. Lena Lennerhed (2005).

9. *Revolution på svenska – ett vittnesseminarium om jämställdhetens institutionalisering, politisering och expansion 1972–1976*. Ed. Anja Hirdman (2005).
10. *En högskola av ny typ? Två seminarier kring Södertörns högskolas tillkomst och utveckling*. Eds. Mari Gerdin & Kjell Östberg (2006).
11. *Hur rysk är den svenska kommunismen? Fyra bidrag om kommunism, nationalism och etnicitet*. Eds. Mari Gerdin & Kjell Östberg (2006).
12. *Ropen skalla – daghem åt alla! Vittnesseminarium om daghemskampen på 70-talet*. Eds. Mari Gerdin & Kajsa Ohrlander (2007).
13. *Makten i kanslihuset. Vittnesseminarium 16 maj 2006*. Eds. Emma Isaksson & Torbjörn Nilsson (2007).
14. *Partnerskapslagen – ett vittnesseminarium om partnerskapslagens tillkomst*. Eds. Emma Isaksson & Lena Lennerhed (2007).
15. *Vägar till makten – statsrådens och statssekreterarnas karriärvägar*. Anders Ivarsson Westerberg & Cajsa Niemann (2007).
16. *Sverige och Baltikums frigörelse. Två vittnesseminarier om storpolitik kring Östersjön 1991–1994*. Eds. Thomas Lundén & Torbjörn Nilsson (2008).
17. *Makten och trafiken i Stadshuset. Två vittnesseminarier om Stockholms kommunalpolitik*. Ed. Torbjörn Nilsson (2009).
18. *Norden runt i tvåhundra år. Jämförande studier om liberalism, konservatism och historiska myter*. Torbjörn Nilsson (2010).
19. *1989 med svenska ögon. Vittnesseminarium om Östeuropas omvandling*. Eds. Torbjörn Nilsson & Thomas Lundén (2010).
20. *Statsminister Göran Persson i samtal med Erik Fichtelius (1996–2006)*. Ed. Werner Schmidt (2011).
21. *Bortom rösträtten. Politik, kön och medborgarskap i Norden*. Eds. Lenita Freidenwall & Josefin Rönnbäck (2011).
22. *Borgerlig fyrklöver intog Rosenbad – regeringsskiftet 1991*. Eds. Torbjörn Nilsson & Anders Ivarsson Westerberg (2011).
23. *Rivstart för Sverige – Alliansen och maktskiftet 2006*. Eds. Fredrik Eriksson & Anders Ivarsson Westerberg (2012).
24. *Det började i Polen – Sverige och Solidaritet 1980–1981*. Ed. Fredrik Eriksson (2013).
25. *Förnyelse eller förfall? Svenska försvaret efter kalla kriget*. Ed. Fredrik Eriksson (2013).

26. *Staten och granskningssamhället*. Eds. Bengt Jacobsson & Anders Ivarsson Westerberg (2013).
27. *Almedalen – varför är vi här? Så skapades en politikens marknadsplats – Ett vittnesseminarium om Almedalsveckan som politisk arena*. Ed. Kjell Östberg (2013).
28. *Anarkosyndikalismens återkomst i Spanien. SACs samarbete med CNT under övergången från diktatur till demokrati*. Ed. Per Lindblom (2014).
29. *När blev vården marknad? Vittnesseminarium i Almedalen*. Ed. Kristina Abiala (2014).
30. *Brinner "förorten"? Om sociala konflikter i Botkyrka och Huddinge*. Ed. Kristina Abiala (2014).
31. *Sea of Identities: A Century of Baltic and East European Experiences with Nationality, Class, and Gender*. Ed. Norbert Götz (2014).
32. *När räntan gick i taket: Vittnesseminarium om valutakrisen 1992*. Ed. Cecilia Åse (2015).
33. *Nordiskt samarbete i kalla krigets kölvatten. Vittnesseminarium med Uffe Ellemann-Jensen, Mats Hellström och Pär Stenbäck*. Eds. Johan Strang & Norbert Götz (2016).
34. *Solidariteten med Chile 1973–1989*. Eds. Yulia Gradskova & Monica Quirico (2016).
35. *25 år av skolreformer – hur började det? Vittnesseminarium om skolans kommunalisering och friskolereformen*. Ed. Johanna Ringarp (2017).
36. *Levande campus: Utmaningar och möjligheter för Södertörns högskola i den nya regionala stadskärnan i Flemingsberg*. Eds. Johanna Ringarp & Håkan Forsell (2017).
37. *Utbildningsvetenskap: Vittnesseminarium om ett vetenskapsområdes uppkomst, utveckling och samtida utmaningar*. Eds. Anders Burman, Daniel Lövheim & Johanna Ringarp (2018).
38. *Pontus Hultén på Moderna Museet: Vittnesseminarium på Södertörns högskola, 26 april 2017*. Eds. Charlotte Bydler, Andreas Gedin & Johanna Ringarp (2018).
39. *AIDS i Sverige: Hivepidemin och rörelserna*. Eds. Kjell Östberg & Lena Lennerhed (2019).
40. *Romerna och skolplikten: Hot eller möjlighet?* Ed. Håkan Blomqvist (2020).

41. *Sweden in Solidarity, Museums in Exile: The Chilean Resistance Museum in Solidarity with Salvador Allende and the International Art Exhibition for Palestine*. Ed. Charlotte Bydler (2022).

42. *Kamp mot droger: En bok om Förbundet mot droger*. Kjell Östberg (2019).

43. *North and South: European Social Democracy in the 1970s*. Eds. Alan Granadino, Carl Marklund & Johan Strang (2021).

44. *Recollections of Joining the EU: Iberian and Nordic Experiences*. Eds. Alan Granadino, Peter Stadius & Carl Marklund (2023).

45. *Visions of the Nordic Model in Northern and Southern Europe (1970s–1990s)*. Eds. Alan Granadino, Andreas Mørkved Hellenes & Carl Marklund (2023).

46. *Sverigebilden i USA: Historia, händelser och mekanismer*. Carl Marklund (2023).

47. *The image of Sweden in the USA: History, events and mechanisms*. Carl Marklund (2024).

www.ingramcontent.com/pod-product-compliance
Lightning Source LLC
LaVergne TN
LVHW040907150826
845672LV00007B/1924

* 9 7 8 9 1 8 9 6 1 5 4 7 2 *